The MBO Deal

The MBO Deal

Inside the management buyout

RICHARD H. WESTCOTT

An imprint of Pearson Education

London ■ New York ■ San Francisco ■ Toronto ■ Sydney ■ Tokyo ■ Singapore
Hong Kong ■ Cape Town ■ Madrid ■ Paris ■ Milan ■ Munich ■ Amsterdam

PEARSON EDUCATION LIMITED

Head Office:
Edinburgh Gate
Harlow CM20 2JE
Tel: +44 (0)1279 623623
Fax: +44 (0)1279 431059

London Office:
128 Long Acre
London WC2E 9AN
Tel: +44 (0)20 7447 2000
Fax: +44 (0)20 7240 5771
Website: www.briefingzone.com
        www.financialminds.com

First published in Great Britain in 2002

ISBN 0 273 65920 0

British Library Cataloguing in Publication Data
A CIP catalogue record for this book can be obtained from the British Library.

10 9 8 7 6 5 4 3 2 1

Typeset by Monolith – www.monolith.uk.com
Printed and bound in Great Britain

The Publishers' policy is to use paper manufactured from sustainable forests.

About the author

Richard Westcott was a prizewinner at the examinations of the Institute of Chartered Accountants and the Fellowship examinations of the Chartered Institute of Taxation. His early career was as a taxation specialist, during which time he spent a period with one of the big five accounting firms and lectured at the Chartered Institute of Taxation conferences. He was called to the Bar in 1978. He subsequently worked in the City for many years as a corporate finance director at Morgan Grenfell & Co. Ltd, and latterly at Warburg Securities and Merrill Lynch. He was involved in many significant corporate finance transactions both in the mergers and acquisitions field and in capital raising. Thereafter he was engaged in consultancy roles where he undertook capital reconstruction projects and acted as a non-executive director of several companies, some of which were listed. One of these companies was Fairview New Homes where he was to become Finance Director, initially on a part-time basis.

While undertaking this role at Fairview he was heavily involved in the demerger of the company from Hillsdown Holdings in 1998 and played a leading role in the management buyout of Fairview from its public shareholders earlier this year. In playing that role he saw the need for this publication. His combination of technical skills and practical experience, not least in the MBO process itself, makes him ideally qualified to write this briefing.

Richard Westcott may be contacted through the publishers.

Contents

Contents

Preface

Having just played the main implementation role within the company in the management buyout of Fairview Holdings Plc, I became acutely aware of the sheer work involved and the additional complexities involved in an MBO. This is despite the fact that I had worked in the City, mainly in investment banking, for almost 20 years until the early 1990s. Indeed, without that and subsequent experience I would have had to rely even more upon advisers. It also became clear to me that little has been written to let the busy business executive, particularly perhaps the finance director, know what he is taking on when he embarks upon the transaction and generally to guide him through the process. An industry has built up over the past decade or more which specializes in management buyouts and certainly the leading practitioners among the legal firms, which are often the medium-sized firms, have written many excellent technical briefings. There is not, however, as far as I am aware, any easily read guide to the subject.

With my recent experiences in mind, I have therefore attempted to write such a guide. It does not set out to be a technical treatise – that is for the professionals – but in it I try to uncover some of the mystique of the subject and try to put the MBO team on a level playing field when it comes to dealing with the professionals and in negotiating the terms of the transaction. Accordingly and inevitably it does contain some technical references, and I have included a glossary of some of the terms which are commonplace to the industry, although many will be known to the reader in other contexts. As will be discovered in reading the book, one of the most important documents in the MBO is the business plan and model, and I am most grateful to UBS Warburg, the leading investment bank, for allowing me to include its draft model as an appendix. If the businessman embarking upon an MBO finds an early read informative and the subsequent study of specific chapters a useful manual of what is involved then I will have succeeded in my task. A few hours reading the book will I hope be a good investment for the hundreds, if not thousands, of hours which will be spent on the transaction itself.

It is also hoped that the book may in itself stimulate further interest in the MBO process and result in an increased flow in transaction volumes to the benefit of shareholders, management, investors and professionals alike.

Introduction

The management buyout of a quoted company is one of the most complex of domestic corporate finance transactions, combining, as it does, a takeover of a listed company with many of the aspects of an initial public offering (flotation) and also the raising of large amounts of debt finance. At the same time the business has to continue to be managed in an efficient manner, particularly as in the public to private transaction (i.e. the purchase from public shareholders of a listed company by its management) the company will continue to be listed until the deal is concluded and will have to continue to publish its half yearly results and comply with all of the other Stock Exchange listing requirements. This places enormous strains upon the management team and it is key that at the outset there is a clear understanding of responsibilities so that the underlying business can continue to function. The chairman and the non-executive directors will, as will be explained later, have a key role to play in ensuring that the pursuit of the management buyout does not detract from the smooth running of the business.

Tensions will at times inevitably run high, not just because of the sheer workload but also because of the various negotiations which will need to be concluded on the terms of the transaction with the non-executive directors on behalf of the existing public shareholders and on the new financing arrangements with the equity house partner and banks. In the former instance one will be negotiating with existing boardroom colleagues and in the latter case with potential ones.

The length of time from deciding to embark upon a buyout to making the first offer may easily amount to four to six months, particularly if there are several banks involved in the financing. This extended timescale will add to the stresses and strains of the transactions.

Once the deal has been completed and the company is in private hands the real work begins as by now the business will be in a highly leveraged structure with the returns available to management being geared to performance criteria. Nonetheless the potential rewards available to management can be enormous and this is what will make the whole effort and transaction worthwhile.

The text, which is based largely upon my experience in the MBO of Fairview Holdings plc, has been produced on the basis of a UK public to private transaction but most of the principles will apply equally to the buyout of a subsidiary from a larger company (where for shareholders and non-executive directors read parent company and its board of directors) or to overseas transactions. The actual provision of the City Code on Takeovers and Mergers applies only to companies in the UK and will not normally apply to the purchase of a subsidiary or group of subsidiaries.

Executive summary

	Setting the MBO in Motion	
Chapter	*Stage*	*Actions*
1	Seek initial outside advice	Discuss with any or all of: ■ company lawyers ■ company auditors ■ investment bankers ■ identified equity providers (if any)
	Determine whether likely to be a viable proposition	■ Prepare draft business plan and model ■ Make general financing assumptions ■ Make assumptions as to offer price for business
2	Move to formal stage	■ Complete appointment of advisory team ■ Split board of company so non-executives negotiate on terms ■ Takeover Code requirements come into play ■ Significant costs likely to begin to be incurred ■ Identify equity house backer ■ Identify bank debt providers ■ Enter into non-solicitation and inducement fee arrangements ■ Commence negotiations on acquisition of business

	The Transaction Process	
Chapter	*Process*	*Highlights*
4	Undertake due diligence	■ Accounting and systems ■ Insurance ■ Legal ■ Commercial ■ Property and valuation ■ Other specialist reports
5	Negotiate banking arrangements	■ Quantum of loans ■ Mezzanine requirements ■ Agree covenants ■ Repayment terms ■ Hedging arrangements
6	Complete business plan and model	■ Description and history of business ■ Market position and prospects ■ Achievability of forecasts

		■ Agree financial projections
		■ Apply financing arrangements to model
		■ Flex model for sensitivities
7	Negotiate legal documentation	■ Memorandum and articles of company
		■ Investment agreement with equity house
		■ Option agreement to acquire equity house's stake
8	Negotiate terms with equity house	■ Agree financial contribution
		■ Agree management incentive, i.e. ratchet
		■ Agree warranties .
		■ Agree board structure
		■ Agree on exit strategy

The Buyout Itself

Chapter	Subject	Highlights
9	Negotiating terms	■ Valuation principles
		■ Comparable companies
		■ Financing limitations
		■ Existing shareholder requirements
		■ Agreement of terms
10	The offer	■ Despatch offer document
		■ Offer timetable
		■ Going unconditional
		■ Buy-in of minority
		■ Whitewash procedure
		■ Giving security

Background to the MBO

INTRODUCTION

During the purple period for technology, media and telecommunication stocks ('TMTs') many solid and capable businesses became unloved by the institutional investors, and with index-tracking and performance measurement criteria being applied by or to investment managers, companies outside the FTSE 100, and certainly those outside the FTSE 350, went 'off the radar screen' as far as the institutions were concerned. In the transaction in which I was heavily involved more than one major institution used that phrase in respect of shareholdings of 3 per cent worth about £10 m. Is it any wonder that managements of basic and smoke-stack industries are weighing up the options open to them when their equity shares are being orphaned by the investment community? Such a situation is demoralizing to management and, if equity is being used in the form of option schemes or other long-term incentive schemes to encourage management and staff at all levels but does not reflect the underlying performance of the business, this may well lead to the despondency and the defection of staff.

It is particularly in this environment that management has reassessed the options open to them and, with the equity of their businesses trading at low levels, considered the management buyout option. Of course, this is not an entirely philanthropic exercise! If the company can be acquired at a sensible price with a reasonable amount of the equity in the buyout vehicle being available to management, then large rewards are potentially available in the short to medium term. Additionally, the regulatory requirements now applicable to listed companies can be cast aside in the letter if not entirely in the spirit. The new corporate governance regime incorporated in the 'Combined Code' following the Cadbury, Hampel, Greenbury and Turnbull reports may now have settled down and have its positive side but it is still onerous as far as smaller companies are concerned. To move forward with the MBO it must be recognized that there will be risks to which management and the business will be exposed. These cannot be ignored and are discussed later.

There are other strategic options which the management team may consider as alternatives to the MBO but these will often be only short-term panaceas. For example, if the company is undergeared and/or has surplus financial resources it will often consider buying in its own shares; this will often increase assets and earnings per share and boost the share price. Except to the extent that management holds equity or options in the company, this will have little direct benefit to management and investor lethargy will soon reappear. Selling off divisions of the company or, indeed, agreeing to a takeover itself will produce value for shareholders but be of little benefit to management and employees who will find themselves, at best, under the control of a new owner or, at worst, without jobs, particularly if there are synergies between the two businesses which result in significant cost-cutting. Going in the opposite direction and acquiring other businesses may raise the company's profile and the attention of investors but will put great strains on management in integrating new businesses without necessarily compensatory financial benefits accruing to management.

Having reached this impasse and having concluded that the pursuit of an MBO is worthy of further consideration, how should management approach the next stage?

THE EARLY STAGES

In most small to medium-sized organizations it is likely that the chairman, chief executive and finance director will have had the early discussion concerning the possibility of an MBO. The next stage is to decide who the MBO executives are likely to be. Human nature being as it is, it is likely that, on the one hand, there will be a desire to keep the team as small as possible so as to maximize possible returns but, on the other hand, it will be vital to both management and the backing institutions and banks (more of which later) to include those executives who are key to the success of the business over the medium term. Certainly, to isolate any such executives to the extent that they vote with their feet and leave will be counter-productive to the whole process. It is also worth pausing to make a couple of critical points:

- As directors of a company the MBO team have a fiduciary duty to the company and its shareholders. They must always act in the best interests of the company and preserve its assets, which include the personnel employed by it. They must not disclose confidential information in respect of the company's affairs without the full consent of the board which crucially includes the non-executive directors who, as will be explained later, have a pivotal role to play as the MBO proceeds. These responsibilities will probably be reinforced in the executive's service contract and any breach of them could give rise to dismissal and legal action.

- If the MBO transaction is to have any chance of success absolute secrecy is paramount. The threats of counter proposals from other trade buyers, let alone the effect on the terms of the deal to be negotiated of a rising share price which in the event is discounting (in market parlance) a transaction, are obvious.

CHOOSING THE EQUITY PROVIDER

Choosing the appropriate provider of the equity finance is the key decision which the management team will have to take before proceeding with the transaction. The choice is key because the equity provider will, in the early years, own a majority stake in the company and will also be the partner of the MBO team in running the business. It is, therefore, critical that the right chemistry exists between the MBO team and the equity house and that they have common goals.

In practice, it is likely that the equity house will be chosen in one of two ways.

Personal contact and recommendation

It is likely that either one of the directors of the company or someone among the company's advisers will have had contact with one of the leading equity house providers. In these circumstances, it may well be that a personal introduction will result in a satisfactory relationship being established, leading to the agreement of the terms on which the finance will be provided. While this may result in an enduring personal relationship between the parties it does suffer from the possible drawback that the optimum financial terms may not have been obtained.

Seeking proposals from several equity providers

If the management team has already appointed either an investment banking adviser or the corporate finance department of its auditors or another leading accounting firm (see below) it may decide that it is best first to produce an initial business plan and model (see below) and then to use these as the basis to seek indications of terms from a number of equity providers. In using a common model there will then be consistency in the basis upon which the equity providers make their proposals. Management can then, at a series of meetings with the equity providers, decide upon which proposal to pursue based upon both the personal chemistry and the attractiveness of the financial arrangements.

The main drawbacks of going this route are probably the added time which it will incur and also the risk that, with more people 'in the know', there will be a greater chance of a security leak of the possible transaction. This is not a reflection on the equity houses but merely a result of widening the circle.

Chapter 3 gives a brief summary of the venture capital industry and details of some of the leading players in the industry in the UK.

TAKING OUTSIDE ADVICE

Once the composition of the MBO executive team has been established and it has been concluded that an MBO should be explored further it would normally be necessary to move to some outside advice. The parties who may be approached at this stage on a very preliminary basis are:

- the company's auditors whose corporate finance departments may be prepared to give initial advice;

- the company's solicitors who, although retained by the company and therefore potentially on the other side of the transaction, will advise on the legal responsibilities and give general guidance;

- an equity backer or venture capital house which will be able to assist in evaluating the financial implications of an MBO transaction and advise whether initial indications show that such a transaction is capable of being viable;

- an investment bank which will be able to perform the same initial work as the equity backer and in due course assist in the selection of an appropriate equity backer or venture capital house if one has not already been identified.

The company's own investment banking advisers will normally be committed to the company and therefore will not be available to advise the MBO team other than in the most general terms.

The management team will often have few liquid resources of their own and will be keen to keep any fees to a minimum. All fees will be a matter of negotiation but many advisers will be prepared to work on a 'no deal no fee' contingency basis in these early stages. This is clearly something which should be the subject of an agreement at the outset to avoid embarrassment later, as many of the advisers' normal charge-out rates will amount to several hundred pounds (sometimes as much as £500) an hour. It is a fact of life in this situation that the clout, support and enthusiasm of an established equity finance house for the transaction may well be critical in obtaining acceptable contingency fee arrangements with other advisers.

THE NATURE OF THE ADVICE

Having decided in principle that an MBO would be an appropriate step, the MBO team will want to make a preliminary evaluation of whether such a transaction is capable of success. MBOs are a form of leveraged transaction. In other words, to be viable to the equity backers (the MBO executives and the equity finance funds) the transaction must be financed by a high level of straight debt usually provided by the major banks, although sometimes refinanced in the longer-term fixed interest market. The underlying business must therefore be sufficiently robust to service such debt in terms of both interest and capital repayments. In order to assess whether this is likely to be the case a financial model, 'the model', will have to be produced which will typically cover the next five to ten years of trading. This is the basis of the advice which will be provided by the retained adviser.

All equity finance houses and the leading investment banks will have their own computer-based models which can produce spreadsheet evaluations of the MBO transaction. Bearing in mind what was said earlier about directors' responsibilities and confidential information, such a model will, in the early stages, have to be produced from publicly available information. Most listed companies will have brokers' research written about them and this, together with earlier published accounts, can be the starting point. The finance director, in his capacity as a member of the MBO team, will be able to apply some general cash flow assumptions, including levels of capital expenditure, to the profit profile.

For example, in the housebuilding industry the land bank is such that the company can have a fairly clear view, in a stable environment, of where the profits are likely to be earned and their level over at least the next three to five years. Indeed, this is the very basis of the management accounts which will be regularly provided to the board. Companies which operate with a reasonable level of glasnost and transparency with the City will often be the subject of research which bears some resemblance to the likely profile. Companies which have shorter lead times in their production cycle or are involved in more volatile industries may find it more difficult to predict their future trading but, nonetheless, will have their own internal forecasts and budgets and these will have been used by management when briefing City analysts on likely trading prospects. Having determined the basis of the model it will be necessary to construct it in the following way:

1. The publicly available forecasts will need to be extrapolated over the period of the model which is likely to be longer than City analysts' estimates.

2. The financing assumptions as to equity, mezzanine (see later) and debt will need to be overlaid onto the trading performance as extrapolated above.

3. An assumption will need to be made as to how the major equity house provider will obtain realization of its equity together with its profit ('the exit').

Once these assumptions have been made and the model produced (in practice being amended several times in the process) it will be possible to assess whether an MBO is likely to be a practical proposition from a financial point of view and, equally importantly, what price should be paid for the business in order to produce the right returns for investors. Such price can then be compared with the valuation of the company on the Stock Exchange and the price which the existing investors are likely to require to sell their shares or to assent them to an offer for the company.

If these preliminary exercises produce a positive indication then the MBO team must take stock and decide whether or not to proceed to the more formal stages of an MBO.

At this juncture it is worth marshalling the factors which the MBO must consider before deciding whether to take this considerable step forward.

- The widening of the circle of people who are aware of the possibility of an MBO to a host of outside advisers and financiers together with the associated meetings and due diligence exercises, many of which will be carried on within the company itself, will inevitably, and despite taking all precautions, increase the risk that the intentions of management will be leaked to the outside world. This is, unfortunately, a fact of life and can both unsettle staff and put the future of the whole company at risk by giving the impression that it is for sale. This must be countered by making it clear that the company is not for sale but is merely considering a proposal from management. Nevertheless, any 'run up' of the share price will increase the expectations of shareholders of a capital realization and, hopefully, a profit. This risk also exists in the case of a sale of a subsidiary as unsolicited higher offers from third-party buyers may be attractive to the parent company.

■ Once a formal offer has been made by the MBO team this places a price on the business which will often be below the price which could be obtained for the business if a full-scale auction were to have been conducted. This is a major risk and unless full commitment can be obtained from shareholders before the announcement of the deal little can be done about it.

■ The consequence of the two points above is that the MBO exercise will normally, at some stage, expose the business to the risk of an offer from a third party. While there have been exceptions, the MBO team will not normally be in a position to match or exceed the third-party approach in terms of either price or speed. Management will be aware of the likely predators, if any, and will be able to weigh up the extent of the risk.

■ It is therefore self-evident that, in attempting to attain the MBO goal, management may be risking the security of their own careers within the company in pursuit of the larger objective. There is no guarantee that if a third party acquires the company, management will be required to remain and, indeed, may not wish to in any event.

■ The MBO team may incur costs to third parties which it will have to settle in the event of an aborted bid. As already noted, many of these may be on a contingency basis which will mitigate the cost. Few of the costs can properly be paid by the target company, these probably being limited to the company's lawyers, its own retained investment banking adviser, its auditors in producing financial information for the offer document and the company's retained financial and PR advisers.

■ Emotions may run high during the MBO process. On the one hand, the MBO team will be negotiating with the non-executive directors (representing the shareholders) who are normally (and may continue to be) their boardroom colleagues. On the other hand, the terms of the arrangement with the equity backers will be a separate negotiation and, if successful, will be with the MBO team's future 'partners' in the venture. Diplomacy will be needed at several points in the negotiations.

None of the above should deter the MBO team as where there are high potential rewards there are always associated risks. Nonetheless, management must go into the exercise with its eyes open and be prepared to weigh up the relative risks.

Management must also be aware that under the Company Securities (Insider Dealing) Act 1985 as amended by the Financial Services Act 1986 they, and subsequently the equity house and Newco (the bidding vehicle), must observe the provisions of the Act and not deal (or give information to third parties to deal) in the shares of the target company when they are in receipt of price-sensitive information (insider dealing). While general rumour may surround the company and the possibility of a management buyout, the MBO team must not add credence to this and cause persons to deal without a general statement to the market as a whole through the official channels. Contravention of the Act is a criminal offence and would lead, at the least, to a fine and, at worst, imprisonment. Advice will need to be taken from the advisers at all stages of the transaction if market purchases are to be contemplated by Newco or its associates to ensure that the insider dealing provisions are not violated.

2

Setting the process in motion

BACKGROUND

In the UK, companies are governed by a unitary board of directors. In other words, the senior board comprises both executive and non-executive directors. If the executive directors form the MBO team then the position arises where the non-executive directors represent the shareholders' interests in the negotiations with the MBO team. This situation is recognized by the Panel on Takeovers and Mergers in its City Code which regulates the takeover of (in the main) publicly listed companies.

Under Rule 3 of the City Code on Takeovers and Mergers the board of the offeree company must obtain 'competent independent advice', the person being appointed to give such advice normally being labelled the 'Rule 3 adviser'. The rule goes on to say that this is particularly important in the case of a management buyout and that the independent adviser must be appointed 'as soon as possible' after it becomes aware of the possibility that an offer may be made.

Rule 25 of the Code goes on to say that the board of the offeree company (in this case the subject of the MBO) must circulate its views on the offer to shareholders together with the advice given by the Rule 3 adviser. A note to the rule states that where a director has a conflict of interest he should not normally be joined with the remainder of the board in the expression of its views on the offer and the nature of the conflict should be clearly explained to shareholders. A further note adds that if the offer is a management buyout or similar transaction a director will normally be regarded as having a conflict of interest where it is intended that he should have any continuing role (whether in an executive or non-executive capacity) in either the offeror or offeree company in the event of the offer being successful.

It is for the above reasons that the first step in the MBO process will be for the board of the company to meet and, formally, to split the board between the MBO team and the other directors, normally the non-executives. The resolution will note the approach of the MBO team to make a possible offer and give consent to the MBO team to enter into negotiations and release information on the company to its advisory team and financial backers. It is essential that until this stage is reached no confidential information passes.

LEGAL AGREEMENTS

It is usual at this point, and as soon as the equity house has been chosen, to ask the non-executive directors to enter into the following agreements on behalf of the target company:

1. A non-solicitation agreement under which the non-executive directors undertake not to solicit offers for the company from third parties or to initiate

such discussions. The reason for this agreement is to reiterate that the company is not for sale and, accordingly, an auction should not develop but, rather, the directors are being asked to consider a proposal from management. The agreement usually also includes an undertaking by the non-executives to advise of any other unsolicited approaches which provides the management team with the opportunity to terminate its discussions so that the board can reunite and defend, if appropriate, any unwanted proposal on its merits.

2. An inducement fee arrangement. The equity house will incur a great deal of time and significant expense in pursuing the proposal. It often requires an inducement fee from the target company in consideration for investigating the possibility of making an offer which will be payable only in the event that an offer is accepted from elsewhere. The fee will then usually be used by the equity house to pay the fees and costs incurred in the abortive process. Because of the financial assistance provisions of section 152 of the Companies Act 1985 the break-up fee which is commonplace in the US and which is specifically to reimburse costs cannot be exactly replicated in the UK and the inducement fee has therefore become the accepted practice. Such inducement fees must be cleared with the Takeover Panel which wishes to ensure that bona fide third-party offers are not frustrated. In such circumstances the Takeover Panel will not normally approve an inducement fee in excess of 1 per cent of the offer value and will require confirmation from the offeree board and its financial adviser that the fee is in the best interests of shareholders. Care will also be necessary to ensure that the Stock Exchange requirements are observed (if applicable) in respect of indemnities if these are capable of exceeding 25 per cent of the average profits of the last three years.

TAKEOVER CODE REQUIREMENTS

Two further significant consequences follow from the resolution to split the board:

1. From the point of view of the City Code the board's obligations are in the hands of the non-executive directors and the Rule 3 advisers. This means that any announcements in respect of the approach, including any required under Rule 2.2(c) of the City Code (which is the case if the company has been the subject of rumour or speculation or there has been an untoward movement in its share price), will be an obligation of those parties, even though in practice they are likely to liaise with the management team.

2. Any information supplied to the MBO equity and financial backers will be the subject of Rules 20.2 and 20.3 of the City Code. Rule 20.2 requires information

generated by the company which has been given to a potential offeror (i.e. the MBO team and its financial advisers) to be made available, on request, to any other bona fide offeror. Rule 20.3 applies only in respect of management buyouts and requires that, on request, the MBO team (as the potential offeror) must promptly furnish the independent directors or the Rule 3 advisers with all information which has been furnished by the offeror or potential offeror to external providers of equity or debt finance.

The purposes of Rules 20.2 and 20.3 are to put any other offeror on an equal footing with the MBO offeror and to give the independent directors and the Rule 3 advisers the same information as provided to the offeror's financiers so as properly to assess the value of the 'business'. In practice, the Rule 20.3 information will need to be handed over and a detailed log of the Rule 20.2 information must also be kept. The finance director and company secretary will have to be particularly rigorous in this even though they may have vested interests elsewhere!

In all other respects the provisions of the City Code apply to an MBO in the same way as they would apply to any other offer.

NEXT STEPS

Now that the board has split and consent has been given for the MBO team formally to pursue the offer, the MBO team will proceed with the following tasks:

1. The formal model and business plan to be provided to the equity and debt financiers will be assembled. This will normally be produced in conjunction with the MBO team's own investment banking adviser or with the equity house providing funds or both (unless the latter has not yet been selected). The basis of the model will normally be the company's own internal budgets and longer-term forecasts adjusted for any relevant new assumptions or criteria which the MBO team wants to introduce.

2. Unless already identified, approaches will be made to and proposals sought from equity houses as to the basis upon which they may be prepared to support the proposal. To facilitate this process the preliminary model will be supplied so that all proposals are based upon the same assumptions and are, therefore, capable of detailed comparison.

3. In conjunction with the investment banking adviser, and possibly the equity house, approaches will be made to banks as potential providers of debt finance.

4. Often it will also be necessary to approach providers of mezzanine finance to bridge any gap between the providers of equity and debt finance. Such providers, being either specialist providers or banks, will require a return

significantly in excess of that required by the debt providers but short of that potentially available to the equity providers.

5. Initial discussions will be opened with the independent directors as to the probable level of the offer. This is likely to be a continuing dialogue between the MBO team's investment banking adviser and the Rule 3 adviser.

Once the model and business plan begins to take shape these can be provided to the equity house or houses and indications obtained as to the basis upon which funds may be provided. This is when the negotiations will begin in earnest. The investment bank chosen by the MBO team will often wish to act for the new vehicle 'Newco' which will be created to make the offer and which will effectively be a joint venture between the MBO team and the equity provider. This may well be a precondition of the investment bank working on a contingency-only basis. It may not therefore be wholly independent in seeking best terms for the MBO team who may wish to appoint their own advisers, unless the MBO team feel confident in their own ability to conduct the negotiations.

PROPOSAL FROM THE EQUITY HOUSE

The main areas on which the MBO team will need to obtain clear proposals in order to choose its equity house partner or to confirm any earlier arrangements are:

- approximate level of offer which the equity house is prepared to support;
- equity to be provided by MBO team;
- equity to be provided by equity house;
- requirements for any mezzanine finance;
- the approximate amount of bank debt necessary to finance the offer;
- the basis upon which the equity house will realize its equity expressed in terms of required rate of return and timing – this is known in the industry as 'the exit' and is discussed in greater detail in Chapter 12;
- the basis of any 'ratchet' available to the MBO team. This is the definition of the basis upon which management's proportion of the equity may be increased, without further investment or cost to the MBO team, if the equity house's return on its investment exceeds certain predetermined rates usually over predetermined time periods;
- the board structure of the offering vehicle 'Newco'.

Once these details have been provided they can be overlaid onto the model to determine the financial rewards available to the MBO team on the attainment of the business plan and model.

It can therefore be seen that the business plan and model is one of the key documents, if not *the* key document, in the MBO process and this will be discussed in much greater detail in Chapter 6.

Having chosen the equity house partner and reached the decision in principle to proceed, several major tasks lie ahead before a formal offer may be launched. These are summarized below and then dealt with in greater detail in later chapters.

BUSINESS PLAN AND MODEL

The business plan and model is key to the transaction as this will:

- provide the basis for the financing; and
- be the basis of a warranty to the banks and equity partners that it is based upon well held beliefs and reasonable assumptions at the date of the offer.

Further work will of necessity be required internally and with the financial advisers before it can be finalized.

APPOINTMENT OF ADVISERS

It will be necessary to complete the appointment of the advisory team which will comprise some or all of the following:

- lawyers to the company (usually the previously retained advisers);
- lawyers to Newco (the bidding vehicle) ⎫ may be the same firm but
- lawyers to the management team ⎭ represented by separate partners;
- lawyers to the equity house;
- lawyers to the banks;
- investigating accountants for due diligence;
- lawyers to report on property titles (if necessary);
- valuers of properties (if necessary);
- investment bankers (or stockbroker) to company (usually existing retained adviser);
- investment banker to Newco;
- public relations advisers to company (usually existing retained adviser);
- public relations adviser to Newco;
- actuarial consultants to advise on the adequacy of pension funding.

The equity house and banks may require other tasks to be completed for which they may appoint advisers (see Chapter 4).

NEGOTIATIONS WITH BANKS AND EQUITY HOUSE

There will be continuing dialogues with these parties during the course of the preparation of the offer culminating in the final negotiations of terms.

PREPARATION OF LEGAL DOCUMENTS

Work will commence on the preparation of the legal documentation, which may differ from deal to deal but will normally comprise:

- investment agreement with the equity house;
- option agreement with equity house for management to acquire its residual shareholding on exit;
- incorporation of and statutory documents for Newco including memorandum and articles of association;
- arrangements for management to make their initial investment, possibly by exchanging existing shares in the company for shares in Newco;
- bank facility documents;
- offer document for the company (in the case of the acquisition of a subsidiary this will be a sale and purchase agreement).

3

The venture capital industry

BACKGROUND

While the equity funds required to finance management buyouts or management buy-ins are not perhaps in the strictest sense venture capital, the venture capital industry has been taken to include such providers and, in some ways, may be seen to be dominated by the major players among the equity capital providers. This is in contrast to the stricter definition of venture capital as the provision of start-up or expansion finance to new or growing businesses. The term private equity has more recently been used to define both forms of capital but would also include, for example, the principal finance operation so successfully run by Guy Hands at Nomura's Principal Finance Group.

This situation is exemplified, for example, by the strong market position of 3i Group plc as a market leader in the management buyout business (it was the main equity provider for Fairview and, more recently, has undertaken the MBO of Go, the low-cost airline on its buyout from British Airways) whereas its roots were in the provision of longer-term finance to industry in its previous guises as the Industrial and Commercial Finance Corporation (ICFC) and the Finance Corporation for Industry (FCI). Indeed, it was set up by the Bank of England and the joint stock banks for this very purpose and only subsequently was it to become an independently listed company and a leading constituent of the FTSE 100.

UK PROVIDERS

Within the UK the providers of equity have evolved over a period of time. The early providers were companies such as Electra Investment Trust, Candover (specifically set up for the purpose) and the Coal Industry Pension Fund through its venture capital arm (which itself was later to be the subject of a reconstruction and rebranded CINVEN when it was acquired by management in 1995). A further early example was Charterhouse Development Capital which was set up by the Charterhouse Group to invest in growing business but which subsequently became involved in the MBO and MBI businesses. Charterhouse's most high-profile transaction was probably the buyout of British Rail rolling stock which was then leased back to British Rail. The business, called Porterbrook, was then sold on to a US trade buyer.

In the last 15 years or so many of the major investment groups and banks in the UK have set up their own private equity arms. Without being exhaustive such operators which have featured in many buyouts in this period have included:

- Legal & General Ventures;

- Phildrew Ventures;

- Schroder Venture Advisers;

- Royal Bank Development Capital;
- Mercury Asset Management (now Merrill Lynch);
- NatWest Equity Partners;
- PPM Venture Managers (formerly Prudential);
- Morgan Grenfell Venture Capital (latterly Deutsche Bank).

There have also been some highly successful independent private equity groups established in the UK. Prominent among these is Apax Partners, established in London by Ronald Cohen many years ago as MMG Patricof & Co. Ltd. More recently Jon Moulton, who had been a leading player in the industry for many years, established Alchemy Partners, which has been involved in some high-profile transactions.

US PROVIDERS

The private equity market also of course had strong origins in the United States and some significant transactions there made players such as KKR (Kohlberg Kravis Roberts) household names throughout the world. The bestselling book *Barbarians at the Gate* by Bryan Burrough and John Helyar (published in the UK by Jonathan Cape in 1990) graphically illustrates the traumas of the most famous transaction of all the leveraged buyouts, RJR Nabisco.

While the US players have undertaken transactions in the UK and Europe their position in the UK has not necessarily been as strong as might have been expected. Equity houses which have become established here include:

- GE Capital Equity Capital Group;
- Kohlberg Kravis Roberts & Co.;
- CVC Capital Partners Ltd;
- Hicks Muse Tate & Furst.

Perhaps the most active of these has been CVC Capital Partners which has been involved in a large number of transactions both in the UK and in Europe. UK transactions include Hamleys and the Gardiner Merchant Group. More recently Hicks Muse Tate & Furst has raised its profile in the UK and was, for example, behind the buyout of Hillsdown Holdings after the latter had demerged its Terranova Foods and Fairview Housebuilding interests; latterly it joined with Apax Partners to acquire the Yell business directory division from British Telecom.

For readers who require an in-depth survey of the private equity business the *Venture Capital Reports Guide to Private Equity and Venture Capital in the UK and Europe* (FT Pitman Publishing) is an excellent reference work.

VENTURE FUNDS

Most of the private equity houses mentioned above raise pools of funds from investor groups to invest in management buyout transactions. In the UK the majority of these funds appear to be of a general nature which can be invested over a range of industries with a consequent spread of risk. On the other hand, in the US, where the market is of course larger, industry-specific funds have been raised particularly to invest in the TMT sectors. Not surprisingly, with the dramatic downturn in these sectors, the returns on some of these funds have come under pressure.

The pools of funds which have been raised by the equity houses will usually have a target closure date by which time investments must be realized and the funds returned to investors. This puts additional pressure on the timetable under which equity investments must be realized by the equity house, i.e. the exit from the investment. If the business which has been the subject of the investment does not perform as anticipated and is not suitable for a Stock Exchange listing, this time pressure may cause other avenues to be utilized, such as the trade sale. These may not be palatable to management but whether the management is or is not the main cause of any shortfall, this is the nature of the private equity market.

4

Due diligence

INTRODUCTION

From the point of view of the equity provider (although there are a few exceptions) and the debt providers, the transaction will be seen as financial rather than as an investment in a business. It will also be seen as a short- to medium-term investment with an exit required within this period. Because of this, the financiers will want to ensure that the business is sound and free from any liabilities, encumbrances or risks which might give rise to any form of embarrassment during the period of investment or inhibit the exit from the business at the end of the period. The equity provider in particular will be keen to establish and corroborate the company's reputation and standing within its industry grouping as well as the competitive advantages and market share which it enjoys. This can be done most easily by a traditional form of SWOT analysis provided initially by the management team. Most of the due diligence will, however, revolve around the financial, economic and legal aspects of the business so that the reports produced by the retained professionals can give the financiers a clear picture of the nature and shape of the business in which they are investing. The equity house and banks will, of course, meet all layers of senior management and visit the company's main operating locations so as to acquaint themselves thoroughly with the business and its people.

Substantial due diligence will therefore be required by the equity and debt providers and may include:

- financial report by accountants into:
  - general review of the business;
  - past results;
  - systems;
  - future projections;
- legal due diligence into constitution of company, contracts and litigation;
- insurance report into sufficiency of insurance cover in place and to be provided;
- property title reports on major properties;
- valuers' reports into value of properties;
- management consultants' reports into management structure and competence of management;
- consultants' report into business processes;
- economic consultants' report into prospects for the industry;
- consulting actuaries' report on the adequacy of the funding of the company's pension fund.

It is evident from the above that there is an enormous amount of work to be carried out while at the same time running the business, the health of which will be vital to any transaction. As far as possible it will be beneficial to place as much of the burden as possible upon the finance director and company secretary, although on some of the commercial issues input will inevitably be required from the other directors.

The due diligence process is one of the most onerous and time-consuming parts of the MBO process. The due diligence necessary is on a par with that which would be needed for a flotation but, rather than just being produced for the sponsors to the issue, in the case of the MBO it will be for the benefit of the equity house and – more particularly – the bank and other debt providers. The various reports produced as part of the process will be the subject of warranties in favour of the equity house and the banks and, in the latter case, breach of such warranties will be likely to give rise to default on the bank loans. The importance of the due diligence is, therefore, self-evident.

The actual due diligence required will necessarily be tailored to the nature and structure of the business so that only a general description can be given, but the areas likely to be covered are detailed in the following sections.

INVESTIGATING ACCOUNTANTS' REPORT

The corporate finance or investigating department of a major firm of accountants will be required to produce a report into the affairs of the target company. This may or may not amount to a normal long form report produced in the case of a flotation. While the report may dwell less upon the history of the business than the flotation equivalent it will be likely to cover some or all of the following areas:

- overview and background of the business;
- legal structure of the business;
- operational structure of the business;
- management structure;
- management succession issues;
- employee profile;
- terms of employment;
- incentive and option arrangements;
- accounting systems – financial and statutory;
- management accounts;
- computer systems;
- accounting controls;
- internal audit;

- organization chart of accounts department;
- forecasting systems;
- reliability of forecasting;
- trading record;
- cash flow history;
- assets and liabilities;
- equipment leasing contracts;
- taxation – including latest compliance position;
- details of pension scheme;
- details of bank facilities and guarantee facilities;
- details of insurance policies and level of cover;
- organization charts;
- curriculum vitae of key personnel;
- details of joint venture arrangements;
- review of the business plan, including the model.

The production of the due diligence reports, and in particular the accountants' report, will place enormous demands on the company's middle management and accounting team. It will also be difficult to maintain secrecy with so many third-party personnel on the premises. Security will be important and code words and project descriptions may be necessary to hold cover as long as possible. The number of those 'in the know' will inevitably expand as the process continues but it should be attempted to keep the team as small as possible.

The part of the report devoted to the review of the business plan and particularly the model will be of critical importance to the banks and the equity house.

The first part of the accountants' review will be to critique the plan and model itself, comparing it to the internal forecasts and budgets already existing within the business and how likely it will be to achieve in relation to the historical performance of the business. The review will also comment on the ability of the business to meet the banking covenants and to repay the bank debt in accordance with the repayment schedule. The level of 'headroom' (i.e. undrawn facilities) will be reviewed throughout the period of the loan and if banking ratios are likely to be breached or reach 'pinch points' at certain stages there is time to attempt to renegotiate these with the banks as all parties will not wish to impose an unworkable straitjacket as long as the model is otherwise constructed on a prudent basis.

The second part of the review will be to apply sensitivities to, or to 'flex', the model to determine the effect on the business performance and model of changes in a variety of factors, for example:

- the economic climate;
- interest rates;
- levels of activity;
- prices and revenues;
- costs.

The outcome of this flexing will assist the management banks and equity house in assessing their particular risks and also in settling the appropriate financing structure. Inevitably the structure will be highly leveraged and thus carry high risks in the early days, but it is important that the structure be robust and sustainable over the period of the plan barring exceptional conditions.

LEGAL DUE DILIGENCE

The other major report to be produced will be the legal due diligence report. This will normally be produced by the solicitors to the buyout vehicle but much information will be forthcoming from the solicitors to the company which in some cases may have produced much of the information for earlier transactions in which the target company may have been involved.

The report will be very wide ranging and the main areas covered will be as follows:

- corporate structure;
- major contracts and contractual relationships;
- banking terms and conditions;
- contingent liabilities;
- regulatory matters;
- litigation – actual and potential;
- terms and conditions of employment contracts;
- employee benefits;
- pension arrangements;
- insurance policies and claims;
- general property matters;
- computer arrangements – software licences, etc.;
- credit licences;
- health and safety issues;
- intellectual property rights;
- property details:
    - lease terms;

- planning arrangements;
- the environment.

It will be noted that there will be some overlap in the areas covered by the accountants' report and legal report although there will be a different emphasis from each discipline.

In becoming involved either as equity owners or as lenders to a leveraged business the addressees of the legal due diligence report will be particularly interested to ensure that they are aware of all potential risks and liabilities and that they are buying into a 'clean business'. The legal due diligence report will also be the subject of warranties by the MBO team.

PROPERTY TITLE CERTIFICATES

If there are several properties owned by the business or if properties form a substantial part of the assets of the business it will often be necessary to obtain solicitors' reports on the property titles in addition to the general due diligence referred to above.

INSURANCE REPORT

As the investors in and the lenders to the MBO transaction will be keen to ensure that the assets of the business are properly safeguarded and are sound from a security point of view, an insurance report into the existing levels of cover will often be commissioned and also on recommendations for the business going forward. In particular, emphasis may be placed upon:

- key man insurance;
- loss of profits and business interruption insurance;
- general adequacy of other levels of cover.

ACTUARIAL REPORT

If the target company operates a final salary pension scheme and if there is no recent actuarial valuation of the scheme it may be necessary to commission such a valuation. In any event, the equity house may wish to receive an independent review of the actuarial assumptions being employed as it will have a vested interest, for the good of staff morale and retention, to ensure that pension assets are safeguarded and the scheme is fully funded.

MANAGEMENT CONSULTANTS' REPORT

The equity house will be taking a highly geared investment in a business in which it is expecting the MBO team to produce both a regular stream of profits and, normally, significant growth. While it will be financially supportive of the business, it will not itself wish to become involved in management beyond the normal non-executive and general investment management roles. Accordingly, it will wish to receive independent corroborative evidence of the quality of the management team and to this end may well wish to ask a firm of headhunters or management consultants to produce a suitable report. This is clearly something which could cause unease among the management team and will need to be handled in an appropriately sensitive manner. It is also likely to be for limited circulation once produced.

ECONOMIC REPORT

The equity house may well commission an independent economic report, particularly if the business is seen to be the subject of business cycles which may be sympathetic to recessionary influences or interest rate movements. While this does not quite fall within the definition of due diligence, any such report will attempt to be as industry and business-specific as possible.

BUSINESS PROCESSES AND EFFICIENCIES REPORT

For reasons already discussed the equity house in particular will be interested in the efficient operation of the business. It may retain a firm of industry specialists or management consultants to report on the efficiency of the business processes and how they compare, by benchmarking if possible, with the best practice in the industry.

Banking arrangements

FACILITIES PROVIDERS

The success or otherwise in being able to launch a management buyout will, to a large extent, be determined by the ability of the MBO team to access the banking markets which are the prime source of finance for such leveraged transactions.

The higher the level of debt which can be raised in respect of the MBO transaction, the higher the potential returns resulting from such leverage. Conversely, of course, the greater will be the risks of failure if trading does not come up to expectations. It is, therefore, critical that an appropriate level of bank finance be raised commensurate with the risk involved in the business. Both the MBO team's investment banking adviser and the equity house will assist in the debt-raising exercise and also in advising on the appropriate debt level. The investment bank may also suggest accessing the high-yield debt market for longer-term debt and in appropriate cases this may also be a sensible course to follow.

The equity house will have several contacts within the banking industry, many of which will have arisen from past transactions. Indeed, it may well suggest that a single major bank will be prepared to arrange and underwrite the whole financing requirement for the deal. This may well give rise to simplicity but may also have its downside factors:

1. The bank may be unknown to the MBO team and in the event that trading becomes difficult may be more difficult to deal with.

2. The bank may well only underwrite the debt rather than retain the whole loan on its own books. This means that a plethora of other banks (both UK based and from overseas) could become bankers to the company. This would exacerbate the problem mentioned in 1 above.

The MBO team may, in the circumstances, be happier to have the banking arrangements provided on a bilateral (one-to-one) basis with their existing relationship banks. While one or two of the UK banks are stronger than the others in the leveraged finance market, all the major banks will normally be prepared to lend monies in the transaction. Even such relationship banks will not undertake not to sell down their loans to third parties as this is not seen to be sensible for prudential reasons but, in practice, they will give every indication that they intend to retain the loans on their own books. As a result of the sheer level of debt involved, the banking terms will be quite strict and the margins required by the banks significantly in excess of those which the MBO team may be used to paying in respect of the business in its current form. This is quite reasonable as it properly reflects the risks which the banks are undertaking. The banks may well be prepared to reduce the margin as the absolute debt level reduces and the banking ratios improve as the transaction progresses.

BANKING RATIOS

Normally, the banks will regulate the loan using the normal banking ratios:

- *debt to equity ratios*, i.e. the maximum level of debt as a proportion of shareholders' funds;
- *interest cover* – this will be the total interest paid in the period compared to the profit before such interest, tax, depreciation and amortization (EBITDA);
- *cash flow cover* – the banks may also compare the level of interest payable, and possibly also the debt repayment projections, to the estimated cash flows arising from the business;
- *loan to value ratios* – where the business has significant assets, particularly real estate, the banks may monitor the loan by reference to the amount outstanding compared to the value of the assets;
- *minimum net worth tests* – this is the figure below which the tangible net worth of the business must not fall.

In the main, however, the banks will be looking at the loans as being serviced both in terms of capital and interest from the cash flow of the business.

OTHER BANK REQUIREMENTS

The negotiations for the bank loans will be protracted and tough and the loan documentation will be considerable, probably running to well over 100 pages. Other than the financial ratios, the requirements of the banks may include the following:

- *Revolving credit facility (RCF) reductions.* These will almost certainly be scheduled reductions in the maximum loan outstanding.
- *Security.* The banks will require a floating charge over the assets of the company and possibly a fixed charge on the real estate assets.
- *Hedging requirements.* The banks will almost certainly require the borrower to enter into some form of hedging arrangement to either fix or place an upper limit on the interest payable so as to limit the risks arising from higher interest rates. Various products exist, such as *swaps* which fix the interest rate at roughly current levels or *caps* which are a form of insurance for which a premium is paid. Such caps limit the increases in interest rates to be paid by the borrower to a predetermined upper limit. Various other hybrid arrangements exist on which the banks will advise and all such instruments have their benefits and disadvantages depending on which way interest rates move. Most interest rate hedging arrangements will have a cost and such cost will have to be incorporated in the financial model. It is often possible to write a cost-free 'collar' under which the borrower places a cap on the

interest rate which he has to pay but at the same time foregoes the benefit of any interest rate reductions below a defined floor. This may, however, be a false economy in the case of an MBO as to forego the benefit of low interest rates (which may only be in place because of a weak economy) may be very costly to the MBO transaction when financial help is most needed. This may also be perceived as a disadvantage of a swap arrangement where the loss of the benefit of a fall in interest rates, particularly in the early stages of the transaction, may give rise to significant extra costs over current interest rates (known as negative carry). The finance director may be content to take his own decision on the hedging arrangements but advice can be obtained from the banks, the investment bankers or specialist advisory firms on the subject. Competitive quotations may be obtained from the banks once the product required has been defined.

- *Key man insurance*. The banks (and indeed the equity house) will require the key members of the management team to effect insurance which will cover at least the cost of the disruption to the business in the event of their early demise or disability.

- *Service agreement*. The banks will want to ensure that the key members of the management team have sufficiently long service contracts to give them security but at the same time have notice periods which are sufficiently short so as not to incur significant cost if the business declines and the banks need to take alternative measures to enforce their security. They will also be interested in the other terms of the contracts, e.g. garden leave.

- *Negative pledge*. The banks will require an undertaking that the company will not pledge its assets or otherwise give any security to any third party during the currency of the loan.

- *Subordination agreement*. There will likely be other debt lines to the vehicle in the transaction, e.g. from the management team and from the equity house. The banks will require an agreement whereby this debt is subordinated (i.e. ranks behind) the bank debt and cannot be repaid until the banks have been repaid in whole or in part.

- *Cash collateral account*. The banks will almost certainly require all trading receipts to be paid into a cash collateral account held by one of their number as a security trustee. This is so that the banks have control over the cash generated by the business in the event of default. As long as there is no default the company will be free to recycle the monies in the normal way.

STRUCTURE OF FACILITIES

The banking facilities will, for technical reasons, probably be structured as a dual revolving credit facility providing for both acquisition advances and working capital advances. This is because, under the provisions of the Companies Act 1985, a company cannot use its own assets to assist in the acquisition of its own shares ('financial assistance'). Once the company is in single ownership there is a provision which enables this situation to be reversed by what is known as the 'whitewash procedure' when the company can be converted from a public limited company ('plc') to a plain limited company and pass the appropriate resolution to give such financial assistance. This procedure is explained in greater detail in Chapter 10.

Under Rule 24.7 of the City Code the banks or the offeror's financial adviser must confirm in the offer document that sufficient funds are available to implement the offer in full ('the cash confirmation'). To meet both this point and the difficulty in obtaining security in the initial stages the banks are likely to structure the transaction in the following way:

- *Certain funds period*. The banks will irrevocably make funds available from the date on which the offer is first announced to the date on which the company becomes fully owned (under the compulsory acquisition procedure) to cover the payments to the public shareholders and the associated costs.

- *RCF – acquisition advances*. The funds to cover the above will usually be the subject of acquisition advances under the revolving credit facility. Initially these will be secured by a debenture on the shares in the target company (the first debenture).

- *RCF – working capital advances*. Before the existing company can give security to its new parent ('the offeror company') for the acquisition advances part of the bank facility, it will need funds to continue running the business. These funds will normally be provided under a working capital advances facility for which security can be given immediately (the second debenture).

Clearly the total funds which can be drawn under the acquisition and working capital advances provisions cannot exceed the limit of the RCF facility. The banks will require an undertaking from the offeror that it will put in place the full security package within a limited time period which will require the offeror to acquire compulsorily the shares of any dissenting shareholders as soon as permitted under the Companies Act. When this and the whitewash procedure have been completed, the third debenture can be given securing the total RCF facility on all the assets of the group.

OPERATIONAL PROVISIONS

The finance director will need to pay particular attention to the operational provisions of the loan documentation as well as to the ongoing information provision requirements. It is he who will be the main point of contact with the banks and who will have to ensure the proper implementation of such provisions. The operational provisions will set out those transactions which can only be carried out subject to the prior consent of the banks and will vary from company to company and be largely dependent upon the nature of the business carried on.

Typical areas covered by operational covenants are as follows:

- capital expenditure levels;
- purchases of businesses;
- sales of parts of the business;
- unusually high levels of trading expenditure, e.g. land purchase for a housebuilder;
- issues of share capital;
- reductions in share capital;
- joint venture arrangements;
- raising of further loans and entering into guarantees;
- entering into leasing transactions.

The information provisions relate to the regular information which will need to be supplied to the banks. While there may be little room for negotiation here it is important that the finance director addresses two principles:

1. Does the information requested correspond to the sort of information already produced and dovetail with the form of management accounts produced by the company? If not, the banks will usually be flexible in agreeing a format which does comply as long as it includes the critical information required.

2. Is the timetable for producing such information reasonable without imposing undue strains upon the accounting function?

If the finance director can clarify these points at an early stage to everyone's satisfaction he will save a great deal of time and energy later in the process.

6

The business plan and model

INTRODUCTION

The business plan and model which must be produced by the MBO team for the use of the banks and equity house is a very comprehensive document upon which the lending and investment decisions will be made. It is therefore a key document in the process and will also be the basis of warranties to be given by the MBO team. It must be prepared with all due care by the MBO team.

THE BUSINESS PLAN

The business plan section will be a narrative account of the business but will also include certain numerical information, mainly of a historical nature. The items covered will normally include:

- a history of the business;
- recent historical financial information;
- performance ratios;
- possibly a SWOT analysis (strengths, weaknesses, opportunities and threats);
- market share information;
- growth prospects of the business;
- a synopsis of the industry in which the business operates and its major competitors;
- the competitive advantages of the business;
- prospects and likely achievability of the financial forecasts.

It is this business plan, together with the model, which will be presented in due course to the investment committees and credit committees – and possibly to the boards – of the equity house and banks to obtain their backing for the transaction. It will also be an important influence on the terms upon which finance is obtained.

The importance of a clear, well presented, comprehensive yet concise document is self-evident and this will be further enhanced if the recent trading record of the group is good. All the providers of finance are backing the management team in relation to the business and its associated business plan and this document, together with the associated presentations and visits to the business locations, provides the real opportunity for management to impress the financiers regarding the quality of the business, its prospects and the management team. Beliefs have to be properly and reasonably held and forecasts and objectives realistic but the importance of the document cannot be stressed too strongly.

The main sections of the business plan are therefore worthy of further consideration.

History of the business

It is important to give details of the original roots of the business and its founders, particularly if the founders are still engaged in the business. If the business was founded to exploit a particular niche in the market then this should also be explained, together with detailed information on how the business has developed since then and adapted to changes in the marketplace. If there have been significant management changes since inception or in recent years, these should be explained in full, particularly to demonstrate, if appropriate, the growth under and strength of the MBO team.

Recent financial information

At least the last five years' trading records of the business should be shown and if there has been a significant change in the constituent parts of the business, the results should be analyzed by showing continuing activities separately from any which may have been sold or closed down. Other non-recurring items should be shown separately, as should financing charges which will be totally changed in a new ownership structure.

While the accountants' report will cover much of this ground it is important that it be summarized here as the decision-makers in the banks and equity house will rely on this document rather than the due diligence reports which more often than not will be studied for exception by more junior staff. The key message to get across in this part of the document is the historical financial performance at a trading level of the business or businesses which are actually the subject of the transaction.

Performance ratios

Among the key ratios which will be of interest to the financial backers are:

- pre-tax profit expressed as a return on equity capital employed;
- pre-interest profits as a return on total capital employed;
- gross trading profits as a percentage of sales;
- net trading profits as a percentage of sales;
- ratio of stocks to sales;
- ratio of debtors to sales.

SWOT analysis

This established matrix of the strengths, weaknesses, opportunities of and threats to the business will give the financiers a useful insight into the risks and rewards which are likely to accrue to the business. If management has not previously produced such an analysis it might also be useful to it in assessing the transaction. The types of matter covered by the analysis will vary from business to business and industry to industry but typical items could be as follows:

- *Market share*. In respect of each defined product area in which the company operates, details of its percentage share of the market and that of its principal competitors should be set out.

- *Competitors – number and relative strength*. Details of each major competitor should be set out with any particular advantages or strengths which each might have over the subject business.

- *Margins*. Do the business products have a high profit margin which is sustainable in the marketplace and available as a buffer in the event of production cost increases?

- *Management strengths*. Any particular strengths of the management team should be set out. These may be, for example, length of time in the industry or innovative or market leadership qualities, or may be as mundane as having weathered significant market downturns or recessions.

- *Size of market*. How large is the market in which the business operates? Is it expanding or contracting? Is there the possibility of increasing market share or expanding geographically?

- *Cyclicality of business*. This would cover the risk to the business of market downturns and the extent to which the business is cyclical and therefore likely to suffer. The effects, for example, of high interest rates or a significant cutback in consumer spending on the business should be spelled out.

- *Capital requirements*. Does the business have a capital-intensive infrastructure? Are the current plant and machinery modern and efficient? If not, or because of rapid technological change, is there likely to be a requirement for high capital spending?

- *Entry costs of competitors*. What obstacles are there and how difficult is it for a new entrant to compete in the marketplace? Are there significant capital and skill requirements which are in scarce supply? Is the lead time to market likely to be offputting? Are the current market participants covered by patents? How difficult is the supply chain?

- *Import substitution*. Is the business vulnerable to currency fluctuations and do these give rise to fluctuations in trading fortunes? Is there a strong overseas supplier base from a low-cost area which gives rise to risks of import substitution, particularly when local currencies are strong?

- *Skill base requirements*. Is the business dependent upon high skills levels which are in short supply? Do such labour pools have a strong bargaining position in times of high demand?

- *Technology advantages.* Does the business benefit from a strong technological base and provide highly engineered and innovative products which competitors struggle to match? Is the business better equipped than its competitors to deal with changes in technology?
- *Strength of brands, patents and trademarks.* Is the product line protected by appropriate patents and trademarks and, if branded, do the products have a strong market position? Is this threatened by own-label products?

Once each of the above matters has been analyzed, it must be categorized as a strength, a weakness, an opportunity or a threat – hence SWOT.

Market share information

The financial backers will be particularly interested in the size of the market in which the business operates and whether it is expanding or in decline. They will also be keen to know whether the business is gaining or losing market share. Recently, major businesses have wanted to be either No. 1 or No. 2 in their markets and this may or may not be feasible for a business which is to be the subject of a management buyout. Niche markets do exist, however, and by positioning itself within a specific subsection of a market a business may obtain major advantages. This section should be written so that the dynamics of the business are clear to the reader.

Growth prospects of the business

This overlaps to some extent with the market share section but will merit a separate section if there are strong prospects, particularly when this needs to be expressed in terms of the technical nature of the markets within which the business operates.

A synopsis of the industry

This section will be relatively brief but will give the reader a broad overview of the industry sector, its degree of fragmentation, the extent to which it is vertically or horizontally integrated, details of the supply chain and markets and the extent to which it is dependent upon particular raw materials or labour markets.

The competitive advantages of the business

Any particular advantages which the business has over its competitors should be spelled out. These may be in one or more different areas, e.g. product differentiation, supply lines or cost advantages.

Prospects and likely achievability of the financial forecasts

The prospects of the business and the achievability of the forecasts contained in the model will be key to the banks and the equity house. Some commentary should, therefore, be provided to put such forecasts into context and to provide some indications of the external factors which could cause those forecasts to be exceeded or missed.

THE MODEL

The model is the financial segment of the business plan. It is the MBO team's assessment of the likely performance of the business over the ensuing five to ten years, although the years which are further out will of necessity be rather broader estimates than the nearer term. On the one hand, the estimated projections will have to be realistic as they will be the benchmark against which future performance will be measured and the subject of warranties to the equity house and banks that they are based upon reasonably held views. (As has been discussed earlier, they will be the subject of detailed scrutiny and analysis by the investigating accountants.) On the other hand, they must present a sufficiently robust picture to enable the financing to be raised.

The information around which the model is likely to be produced probably already exists within the company. The starting point will be the existing budgets for the current and possibly next financial period. It is likely that there will also be in existence a three- or five-year plan. From this information the management team will begin to assemble the trading information part of the model. The budgets and forecasts will be reviewed and conclusions drawn as to the most likely outcomes. The time horizon will also probably have to be extended to stretch the projections out to six to eight years and possibly longer. At the longer end, obviously less reliance can be placed upon the figures but nonetheless they should portray a trend and may well give rise to further questions, for example how can such growth be achieved or what resources, both human and financial, will be required to achieve the results. The trading results can then be supplemented by cash flow forecasts which will reflect the capital expenditures required to produce the results. All of the above information will be available from within the company and the initial model will normally be produced by the finance director with his senior accounting team after having agreed the main assumptions with his MBO colleagues.

The next stage of the process will probably be carried out in conjunction with the investment bank adviser which will have its own MBO model and the expertise to superimpose the financing arrangements onto the more traditional projections produced by management. The model will be far more sophisticated than that produced by management and will show the effects of the debt structure and the required return of the equity house on the business. The model will incorporate all the banking ratios and debt repayment schedules so as to show the areas where the business may come under pressure or, indeed, in the early models, show breaches. For illustrative purposes UBS Warburg has kindly agreed that a draft of its MBO model be included as Appendix 2 to this book.

The main work to be undertaken in completing the financial model from the company's own forecasts can be summarized as follows:

- *Financing*. The broad assumptions being used for the financing, for example, as between equity, subordinated debt (quasi equity), mezzanine finance and straight debt, including any proposals to convert subsequently some bank debt to longer-term bonds, will be built into the forecasts. In the early years this will be done on a monthly basis so that profit and loss accounts, balance sheets and cash flows are available which show where the peaks and troughs in borrowings occur and provide the necessary ratio tests at the end of each month. Once the business is forecast to be well within its covenants the figures can be produced on a quarterly basis thereafter.

- *Interest*. Interest payments will be built into the cash flow forecasts and profit and loss accounts to reflect the contractual arrangements. While the banks will require interest payments on a regular and frequent basis the equity house may only require to be paid interest (albeit at a higher rate) on a six-monthly or annual basis. This longer profile will give the business a little breathing space in its early years when cash flows are usually tight.

- *Dividends*. The equity house will normally be entitled to a dividend based on the profits of the year and this will be shown as a cash flow item on its due date as well as an accrued reduction in reserves in the relevant balance sheet. Management will not normally be entitled to a dividend on its equity until the equity house has had its investment redeemed.

- *Debt repayments*. The debt repayments to both the banks and the equity house and mezzanine providers will be shown in the model on their scheduled due dates in accordance with the loan and investment agreements. If repayments depend on certain ratios or hurdles being attained then the payments will be included as and when the model shows that such points have been reached. There will, therefore, be consistency between the trading assumptions and the terms of the financing.

- *Balance sheet structure*. It is likely that the business will have been purchased at a price which varies from the net asset value of the business – normally a premium. Under normal acquisition accounting rules this will result in goodwill arising on consolidation and this will have to be incorporated in the model and amortized. Similar amortization will need to be included for the expected expenses and costs of the transaction to the extent which these are not written off on acquisition. As noted in Chapter 11 on taxation, to the extent that such costs relate to the raising of finance, amortization will be the correct treatment.

- *Profit and loss account.* Lines will be drawn on the profit and loss account to show profit before interest, tax, depreciation and amortization ('EBITDA'), profit before interest and tax ('PBIT') and profit before tax ('PBT'). The banks and equity house relying mainly upon cash flows will usually regard EBITDA as the most relevant figure and interest covenants, if any, will often be set by reference to this definition.

- *Ratios.* The model will show the main ratios under which the business will be required to operate and these will be shown in respect of each period to determine whether a breach is likely to occur and the extent of any headroom. The main ratios are likely to be:

  - *loan to value ratio* – the ratio of outstanding loans to the asset value of the business;

  - *EBITDA* – expressed as a multiple of interest payable;

  - *total debt* – expressed as a multiple of EBITDA.

- *Headroom.* The model will also show the headroom available at any particular time, this being the excess of the facilities available, taking into account covenant limits over the drawn amounts.

- *Revaluations.* In those instances where finance has been raised by reference to the market value of assets the model will have to incorporate such valuations so as to be able to calculate the appropriate loan to value ratios. Such valuations, particularly where they relate to trading assets, will not normally be incorporated in the company's accounts – such calculations will be of a supplementary nature and will have to be calculated throughout the period of the loan that such valuations exist.

- *Internal rates of return.* The model will show the internal rates of return achieved by the various investors on their investment if the forecasts are met. This is of particular relevance to the equity house which will have a target rate to achieve on its investment, and also to management whose ability to trigger a further share of the equity by way of the ratchet will normally be determined by a hurdle level of internal rate of return.

Once the model has reached a reasonably advanced stage of preparation management will review it in conjunction with the investment bank, the equity house and the banks in a series of discussions with a view to ensuring that any difficulties thrown up can be ironed out by either changing the proposed terms of the transaction or by improving the trading or capital expenditure profile of the business, always of course within the bounds of reasonableness. As has been explained above, the model will have particular regard to the headroom available within the banking and other facilities at any particular time by comparing the actual amounts drawn down with the total facilities available. None of the parties to the transaction – not least the banks – will want to embark upon a transaction that appears to be flawed from the outset, and the equity house and the management team will not wish to have imposed upon them a straitjacket which gives little room for flexibility or is not able to accommodate modest changes in trading fortunes, particularly in the early years.

Having gone through the above procedure and having amended the model several times, a base case model will be produced which in due course will be annexed to the investment agreement and bank facility documents and be the subject of appropriate warranties. While the model is management's document, the equity house and the advisers will give substantial helpful advice and suggestions as to what may be possible, drawing upon their wealth of knowledge of and experience in the management buyout process.

It is likely that several other models will also be run to show the sensitivity of the base case to changes in economic fortune both of the economy as a whole and of the specific business. These sensitivities will be discussed with all the relevant financiers so that as many contingencies can be dealt with as possible within the structure, and so that the financiers are aware of the effects of such changes when they assess the risk profile of the financing arrangements.

In conclusion, it must be emphasized that while the projections and model may be produced by the finance director, his team and the external advisers, the model itself is the responsibility of the whole management team who must 'buy into it' if the management buyout is to have any chance of success. If the management buyout is to be a long-term success it will be key for the projections in the model to be met, especially in the early years. Experience has shown that, with the high financing costs of the MBO, any significant shortfall in performance in the first couple of years will be difficult, if not impossible, to make up later, particularly to a level where the management team can take full advantage of the ratchet.

The legal documents

The legal documents which are normally prepared and/or executed in an MBO transaction are discussed in the sections which follow.

MEMORANDUM OF ASSOCIATION OF NEWCO (THE BIDDING VEHICLE)

This will be standard in its form and the company's objectives will normally be widely drawn.

ARTICLES OF ASSOCIATION OF NEWCO

Particular provisions which will be included in the articles are as follows:

1. *Share capital*. Normally the ordinary share capital will be divided between A ordinary shares and ordinary shares. The equity house will usually hold the A ordinary shares (on which dividends will be paid) and the management will own the ordinary shares which will not normally be entitled to dividends prior to the exit.

2. *Ratchet provisions*. There will often be provision for the ordinary shareholders to increase their share of the equity if the equity house receives a predetermined rate of return on its investment. This is normally done by the equity house ceding part of its holding of A ordinary shares, usually by converting the shares so ceded into worthless deferred shares.

   The ratchet will normally be triggered on a flotation (IPO) or trade sale but other circumstances may be specified in certain transactions.

   There will usually be a longstop date by which the ratchet must be triggered, otherwise it will fall away.

3. *Pre-emption rights*. These are the normal provisions under which any selling shareholder is required to offer the shares to the other shareholders on the same terms as are being offered by a third party before they can be sold to such third party.

4. *Transfer of control provisions*. These are provisions whereby:
   - if control of the company is to pass to a third party, this can only occur if an offer is made on the same terms to acquire the remaining shares on the same terms ('tag along rights'); and
   - if the holders of a majority of the share capital (and possibly a minority held by the equity house after the ratchet has been exercised) desire to sell their shares to a third party then the rest of the shareholders are bound to sell on the same terms ('come along rights' or 'drag along rights').

These latter provisions are included particularly to protect the investment of the equity house which will not wish the liquidity of its investment to be in any way impeded.

INVESTMENT AGREEMENT

This agreement will be between Newco, the promoters (i.e. the MBO team) and the equity house and any other investors. As the name implies the agreement will set out the basis of the equity house's investment in Newco. This will be divided between equity share capital and loans and the agreement will detail the basis upon which the loans are to be repaid (the repayment schedule).

Other provisions normally included in the investment agreement will be as follows:

- number of directors to be appointed by the equity house via its A ordinary shares;
- any additional observers to be appointed by the equity house or investor group who will be entitled to attend Newco board meetings and receive the relevant board papers;
- provisions on the limitations on the expansion of the business (often by reference to the bank loan agreements);
- other provisions on the conduct of Newco and its business, for example:
  - major decisions to be taken at properly constituted board meetings;
  - undertakings to protect the company's assets and intellectual property rights;
  - undertakings to insure the company's assets;
  - undertakings to enforce terms of employment contracts;
- undertakings to provide regular information to the investors and to produce annual business plans;
- undertakings not to take certain actions without the consent of the equity house, for example:
  - not to amend the business plan;
  - not to incur expenditure not included in the business plan;
  - not to create mortgages or charges;
  - not to enter into joint venture arrangements;
  - not to incur borrowings in excess of certain pre-agreed limits;
  - not to capitalize reserves;
  - not to pay salaries to management in excess of the terms of service contracts;
  - not to enter into contracts outside the ordinary course of business;
  - to limit the amount of political and charitable contributions;
  - not to change the auditors of the company.

A further critical part of the investment agreement which will be of particular interest to the management team will be that dealing with warranties. The warranties which the equity house will normally require will cover the following areas:

- the accuracy of the due diligence reports;

- the accuracy of the business plan and model and the fact that the model has been properly compiled based on fair assumptions which have been considered reasonable by the management team;

- the accuracy of the accountants' report and the report and accounts of the target;

- the accuracy of the information supplied by the management team to the equity house in respect of themselves. This will normally cover directorships, other business interests, interests in the target company, other investments, contracts with the company and any convictions other than trivial motoring offences;

- that the formal offer document for the target company is true and accurate in all material respects and not misleading.

As discussed elsewhere, financial limits will be negotiated in respect of total liability under these warranties and a threshold limit for claims.

It will be normal in respect of these warranties, and also those in the banking arrangements, for the management team to provide a 'disclosure letter' against the warranted information. Such items which have been disclosed against cannot then be the subject of claims under the warranties.

SUPPORT AGREEMENT

This is a document which is between the equity house and the bidding company (Newco) and its subsidiaries which will comprise the whole of the target group under which the subsidiaries agree to provide the parent, subject to the terms of any banking agreement, with sufficient funds for the parent to meet its obligations in respect of the loans received from the equity house.

OPTION AGREEMENT

This is an agreement between the equity house and the MBO team under which the MBO team, either for themselves or through Newco, have the right to acquire all or part of the shareholding of the equity house over a specific time at a predetermined price. If exercised, such an option will increase the MBO team's percentage share of the equity in the company. Because of the fixed, and probably somewhat beneficial, price at which the MBO team may be able to acquire the shares under the option, the agreement will usually contain a 'no embarrassment' clause whereby a proportion of any profit accruing to management on the sale of their shares within a specified period will be payable to the equity house.

The negotiation and structure of the transaction

LEVEL OF BANK DEBT

Once the due diligence is under way and the production of the business plan and model has reached an advanced stage, the management team and the equity house will need to agree on the principal terms of the transaction.

Both the management team and the equity house will wish to include as much debt as possible in the structuring of the transaction so that, as holders of the equity share capital, they can take advantage of the high leverage to maximize their returns. The corollary, of course, is that if the business does not perform according to plan this will put the financing structure at risk – a matter which will be discussed later.

The negotiations with the bank, or banks, will determine the maximum amount of debt which can reasonably be accommodated within the projections contained in the model. The management team will also need to be comfortable with these debt levels both in terms of principal amounts outstanding and also the level of potential interest costs against projected profit levels and cash flow. It is not possible to be dogmatic and lay down specific ratios as these will vary from business to business and the relationship between operating profits and available cash flow. The nature of the planned exit by the equity house will also be of some relevance. In the early years, however, it may be that interest costs will only be covered by pre-interest and tax profits two or three times.

MEZZANINE FINANCE

Once the approximate level of bank debt (senior debt) has been determined it will be possible to see what further financing requirements are needed. The equity house will have produced provisional terms as to the amount which it is prepared to commit to the transaction and it will also indicate what, on the basis of its commitment, it would expect management to contribute. If there is an unsatisfied balance of funds necessary to complete the transaction then other sources of finance will need to be approached.

At this stage of the negotiation great reliance will be placed upon the investment banking adviser's estimate of the price which will need to be paid to acquire the company and, particularly in the case of a public offer, this will be a moving target until terms are finally agreed. This is discussed in further detail later.

Based upon the estimate of the total funds required, approaches may need to be made to other institutions to bridge the gap. The senior debt lenders (i.e. the banks) will typically not be prepared to see further funds raised which rank alongside their own lending as this would be seen as diminishing their security in the event of the loan being called and also as weakening the general debt ratios. The approaches will therefore have to be to providers of more junior debt – normally to 'mezzanine debt' providers. Such mezzanine providers will usually be prepared to lend funds which rank behind the senior debt in return for a higher coupon (i.e. interest rate) together, often, with an equity kicker (i.e. a share in profits). Whether they demand an equity return or not such mezzanine providers will certainly be looking for a return significantly in excess of that provided to the senior debt providers.

FINALIZING THE DEAL WITH THE EQUITY HOUSE

Once the general parameters of the debt structure have been agreed these can be overlaid onto the final drafts of the financial model (including the accounting implications of the acquisition) to ensure that the structure is viable. Assuming this to be so, negotiations can begin in earnest between the management team and the equity house to conclude the terms of the deal between them. The major areas where final agreement will need to be reached are:

1. total contribution of the equity house;

2. total contribution of the management team;

3. initial percentage of equity available to the management team, the balance being held by the equity house;

4. the actual total amount of equity. This can be determined once item 3 has been settled. The balance of the contribution of the equity house and the management team can then be provided by way of junior debt;

5. the amount of equity to which the management can be ratcheted if certain performance targets are met and the negotiation of those performance targets;

6. the return on the junior debt provided by the equity house. While the equity house will receive an equity dividend on its shareholding it will look for a large part of its return to come from a high interest rate on the junior debt element of its investment. The interest rate will usually be set at a level which is sustainable from a risk point of view so as to maximize the chances of Newco obtaining a tax deduction for such interest. This is discussed in greater detail in Chapter 11 dealing with taxation;

7. the likely timing and method of exit of the equity house;

8. the level and nature of the warranties to be given by management;

9. the negotiation of the detailed terms of the legal documents which have been discussed in the previous chapter;

10. the basis of the board representation of the equity house and the identification of the equity house's nominees. It is important that there be a harmonious boardroom from the outset if the transaction is to be a success.

Many of these items will have been considered in detail in choosing the equity house (see Chapter 2), but as the final terms of the transaction are concluded (i.e. model, price and financing) there are bound to be changes.

Items 5, 7 and 8 deserve further attention and are considered below in more detail.

THE RATCHET

The percentage of equity which is to be provided to management at the outset, management's initial contribution and the percentage of equity to which it may be ratcheted, including the relevant performance criteria required to do so, are key issues for management. If proposals have been received in the early stages from several equity houses (or indeed from only one) then this should be seen as initial indications against which subsequent negotiations can take place.

Normally the equity house will be prepared to cede under the ratchet a further percentage of equity to management depending on the internal rate of return which it obtains on its investment. The equity house will normally have a target rate of return of at least 20 per cent and probably higher. If that return is not reached then management will not be awarded any further equity through the ratchet mechanism. If, however, that return is exceeded management will receive either a fixed amount of further equity or an amount graduated by reference to the amount by which the base equity return is exceeded.

As can be seen the amounts which management are required to invest and the amount and structure of the ratchet will be vital in determining the ultimate returns available to management.

THE EXIT OF THE EQUITY HOUSE

The equity house will normally be a fairly short-term player which will want to see its investment realized and return crystallized over a three to five-year period. There are three main ways by which the equity house may achieve this 'exit'. They are considered in greater detail in Chapter 12 but may be summarized as follows:

■ *A flotation (or IPO).* By this method the business will continue to be developed and expanded with a view to obtaining a listing on a recognized stock exchange. When the listing occurs the equity house will sell all or part of its holding and management may realize some of its investment also. If the business remains heavily geared at the time of the listing additional funds may have to be raised by the issue of new shares by the company to reduce its debt level. The ratchet will come into play at this stage.

■ A *trade sale*. Under this alternative the business will be sold outright to a trade buyer and the proceeds divided between the equity house and management after adjusting for the effect of the ratchet. A trade sale will often not be the preferred method to enable the equity house to exit as management will normally wish to continue to run the business and participate in its continued growth. With a trade sale the management continuity may not be assured and, in any event, the management would be operating as managers of a subsidiary of a larger organization. This alternative will often come into play if the business has not operated as successfully as indicated at the time of the MBO and consequently profits may be lower and debt levels higher than anticipated. Accordingly, the business may not be considered suitable for a listing and it may be difficult to obtain sponsors to such a transaction.

■ A *recapitalization*. A third and less common way in which the equity house may exit is by way of a recapitalization. Under this arrangement management would further leverage the business to acquire the remaining investment held by the equity house after the ratchet had been triggered. Such a transaction may be pursuant to the terms of an option agreement between the management team and the equity house entered into at the outset. Such a transaction amounts virtually to an MBO on an MBO and may put considerable strains upon the business in terms of the sheer level of debt burden and repayment. It will also mean that management must wait longer to receive a return on its investment and will add to its risks. However, the compensation is that the business will now be wholly owned by management to whom all future profits will accrue. In return for giving the management team the option to acquire the business the equity house will require a 'no embarrassment' clause in the agreement so that it will receive a share of any profit made by the management should they decide to sell or float the business shortly after exercising the option, the terms of which may have been beneficial to management.

WARRANTIES TO BE GIVEN BY MANAGEMENT

The equity house will normally approach the transaction as a financial one in which, as already indicated, it will intend to make its profit and obtain its exit over a relatively short period. With this end in mind, its approach will be to ensure that the business is entirely 'clean' and as free of unforeseeable risks as possible. The due diligence reports will be the basis upon which the equity house (and, indeed, the banks, which will have a similar philosophy) will form this view but in addition the equity house will require appropriate warranties from the management team.

The warranties will be required as much to 'focus the mind' of management so that all information and risks are disclosed as they are required to provide financial compensation. Indeed, management will normally have few assets other than houses, which are probably mortgaged, outside the business so that if things go wrong few funds will be available and little will be gained by pursuing management to the bankruptcy courts. The practice of the main equity houses is not to pursue claims on warranties unless there is some form of fraud or wilful default involved, although when signing any legal warranty management should not rely upon this! A legal commitment is a legal commitment.

The main arguments around the warranties will be their nature and their financial extent. This will be a normal commercial negotiation, with the equity house requiring all the due diligence reports and the business plan and model to be warranted in full. The warranty would be that the documents are correct and, in the case of the business plan and model, that they were based on opinions reasonably held. Sometimes it will be difficult for management to warrant third-party reports which themselves express opinions and which contain diagrams, graphs and pictorial images. With the limited time available to verify these aspects and the other demands upon management time, attempts may be made to limit the warranty to information supplied, although this may well be resisted. The financial limits will be a matter of negotiation and will bear some relationship to some or all of the following matters:

- the size of the transaction;
- the existing stake of management in the business, some of which they may encash as part of the MBO;
- management's investment in the transaction;
- management's other assets outside the business in so far as is known to the equity house.

The sooner that these issues can be settled the better, as management and the equity house will then have the common objective to conclude the acquisition of the business and move forward together to make it a success.

There is a further matter which will need to be dealt with at this stage: the terms upon which management will invest in the business and the return which they are likely to receive will need to be cleared with the Takeover Panel. This is because it is a general principle of the City Code (No. 1) that in a takeover transaction all shareholders must be treated similarly. The Takeover Panel jealously guards this provision and will want to ensure that management are not obtaining any undue advantage not available to other shareholders. The very fact that the management team are shareholders in the bidder (Newco) is obviously something not available to other shareholders but this is because the management team have been proactive in initiating the transaction. The Takeover Panel accepts this and will also usually accede to management being able to switch any investment in the target company into shares and securities of Newco which may provide taxation benefits (see Chapter 11). Early clearance of such issues with the Takeover Panel is to be advised so as to avoid last minute delays and frustrations if there are indeed any complications with the arrangements.

Rule 16 and note 4 to that rule further supplement General Principle 1.

The acquisition of the business

INTRODUCTION

At the same time as the structure of the transaction and the financing arrangements are being put in place, the other major negotiation which will have to be undertaken is for the acquisition of the target business itself. In this management and the equity house will be acting together through Newco with their investment banking advisers to agree terms with the Rule 3 adviser retained by the non-executive directors and then to make the public offer. This will be a negotiation similar to any other between the advisers in a public situation and will dwell upon the valuation of comparable companies, price earnings ratios, asset values and profit forecasts (see below). However, it will be, to an extent, different in one important respect in that the non-executive directors will normally have entered into a non-solicitation agreement (see Chapter 2) not to actively seek, solicit or encourage third-party bidders and will be anxious not to isolate themselves from the management team, the loss of which would leave them in a difficult position. Nonetheless, and despite their difficult position, the negotiation will be a commercial one, albeit without an auction, and, in practice, this is a responsibility which the non-executive directors carry out in a proper manner in conjunction with their advisers. It is inevitable that there will be stresses, strains and frustrations in the course of the discussions but in the main they should be carried out in a dignified manner.

COMPARABLE COMPANIES

The basis of the price negotiation will centre around comparable companies in the field and their relative valuations. The shape and funding of two companies is never identical and while the adviser to the target will tend to be biased towards those with a relatively high valuation, the advisers to the MBO team and equity house will tend to find sound reasons why these are not directly comparable and be inclined towards those with lower valuations. For example, a company which has not reinvested in fixed assets in recent times may be less efficient but nonetheless find its shares trade at a significant premium to its net asset value whereas those of a company with more modern equipment may trade closer to the net asset value.

The type of factors which the respective advisers will consider will therefore be as follows:

- *Net asset value of the company*. How does the net asset value of the company compare with that of its peer group, and is the price being proposed justified by reference to such value? Is there a case for assets which have been owned for some time to be revalued to market value which will compare favourably with the price proposal?

- *Price earnings ratios.* The historic and prospective price earnings ratio which the proposed purchase price represents, based on the previous and forecast current year profits, can be calculated and compared to the price earnings ratios of comparable companies trading on the Stock Exchange. One would normally expect an offer for a company to represent a significant (say at least 30 per cent) premium to the price earnings ratios of currently listed comparable companies.

- *Profit forecasts.* If the target company is internally forecasting a significant increase in profits for the current and future years then this will be taken into account, usually on the basis that this justifies a higher price earnings ratio. In certain cases, the current year forecast may appear in the offer document and be reported upon by the financial advisers so that the shareholders can form their own judgement based on the adviser's recommendation.

- *Premium to current share price.* This may well, in practice, be the most critical factor in obtaining the recommendation of the adviser to the target as the adviser will not give his recommendation to an offer which is likely to fail due to being insufficient. Furthermore, both sides to the negotiation will want to ensure that the shareholders accept the offer, which they are unlikely to do unless there is a sufficient premium to encourage them to do so.

CONCLUDING THE NEGOTIATION

The reality is that, as with all negotiations, it will be a horsetrade to ensure that both sides feel comfortable with the result. If the premium required by shareholders is such that the calculated premium to net asset value and comparable price earnings ratio are excessive, then it is unlikely that the MBO team will want to proceed or that it will be viable to do so. It is perhaps this limit on financing which will often bring realism to a transaction and cause the target company's board and its shareholders to recognize that, if they want the transaction to proceed, there is a price range beyond which the status quo will prevail.

Management and the equity house will wish to acquire the business as cheaply as possible and, indeed as explained above, there may well be financial parameters beyond which they cannot, or will not be prepared to, go. The Rule 3 adviser and the non-executive directors will obviously be trying to obtain as high a price as possible and may be the subject of criticism or general dissatisfaction from shareholders if they recommend too low an offer. It is, however, the shareholders who will have the final say and they will have been consulted by the non-executive directors and Rule 3 adviser during the negotiations as to their likely expectations. Those who do express dissatisfaction often will have sold shares at lower levels in the past and will not have been prepared to invest at modest price earnings levels which will have contributed to any past poor performance in the shares. At a realistic level, most institutions will be sellers and pleased to rid themselves of an illiquid stock which is beneath their radar screen and probably in an old economy industry.

There are two further reasons why the management team and equity house will wish to reach a reasonable level of negotiated offer with the non-executive directors.

- Firstly, to obtain full ownership of the target, Newco will have to gain acceptances from holders of at least 90 per cent of the shares which are the subject of the offer. If this is achieved the balance of the shares can be acquired compulsorily under the provisions of sections 429 and 430 of the Companies Act 1985.

  It will normally be a condition of the banking arrangements that this level be reached so that the provisions can be invoked.

  While there are other ways to approach the offer, e.g. a Scheme of Arrangement under section 425 of the Companies Act, this is not normally to be recommended as it is more ponderous and may be seen by some institutions as a form of coercion.

- Secondly, the management team will be anxious not to put the company into play by putting a price on the company in the form of an offer which has been recommended by the non-executive directors, but which could still be thwarted by a higher offer from an unsolicited third party. In practice, management will be aware of who the potential alternative offerors may be and tentative overtures may already have been made. This gives rise to added uncertainty and, as with any takeover bid, attempts will be made to minimize the risks. To move with complete secrecy and all haste before the offer is announced is usually the best approach but an additional step which can be taken is to obtain undertakings from the major shareholders, if possible holding over 50 per cent of the shares, to accept the offer. The strongest form of undertaking is an irrevocable one which will only fall away if the offer lapses, but institutions may be reluctant to give such an undertaking in the absence of a 'knock-out' offer. Weaker forms impose a time limit after which they fall away and others may allow the giver of the undertaking the right to accept a higher offer if it exceeds the existing proposal by a certain percentage, e.g. 5 or 10 per cent. Such undertakings can certainly minimize the risks and put off the counter bidder but until the offer is declared unconditional even the existence of such undertakings does not guarantee security.

It may be necessary for management to produce a formal profit forecast for the current year in the offer document if this is required by the non-executive directors and Rule 3 adviser. This will have to be reported upon by the Rule 3 adviser and the company's auditors in the normal way.

Conducting the offer and closing the deal

ANNOUNCING THE FORMAL OFFER

While the negotiations are continuing with the equity house, banks and the investment bankers advising the target company, the investment bankers and lawyers to Newco will be preparing the press announcement which launches the formal offer and the offer document which will be sent to the target company shareholders. Once terms have been agreed and the investment bank and/or banks to Newco are able to give the confirmation under the City Code that the funds are available to pursue the bid, the formal offer can be announced, ideally with the public support of as many of the target company's shareholders as possible from whom irrevocable undertakings have been sought. Advisers will usually wish to proceed with the posting of the formal offer document as soon as possible so as to keep the public exposure of the transaction to an absolute minimum. As has previously been explained this is to attempt to reduce the risks of any third-party intervention in the transaction. While there have been exceptions it is most unlikely that if a third-party trade buyer intervenes, the management team will be able to continue to compete in terms of time, resources and flexibility unless it has very secure undertakings from a large group of the target company's shareholders.

Management must be aware that once announced an offer must be capable of implementation in full (Rule 2.5(a) of the City Code). Neither is it possible to include subjective conditions within the offer so as to give the opportunity to withdraw at a later date (Rule 13 of the City Code). Management and their advisers must therefore be confident of the position before they proceed to the formal announcement of the offer.

THE TIMETABLE FOR THE OFFER

The offer itself will be conducted under the provisions of the City Code on Takeovers and Mergers and detailed advice will be forthcoming from the investment banking advisers who have a duty to ensure that they are complied with. There are nonetheless some critical dates and time periods enshrined within the Code that management will need to consider in the tactical approach which it takes to the offer. These are:

- the offer must initially be open for acceptance for 21 days from posting the offer document;

- in the absence of a competing offer the offer must be declared unconditional (i.e. be completed) or must lapse by the 60th day of posting;

- after the 42nd day from posting shareholders who have already accepted the offer may withdraw those acceptances if the offer is not already unconditional.

DECLARING THE OFFER UNCONDITIONAL

Management and the equity house will want to proceed with all due haste to declare the offer unconditional and will certainly wish to do so by the 42nd day so as not to risk losing acceptances which have already been secured. If a third party were to intervene it would certainly try to exploit this provision and canvas shareholders to withdraw their acceptances and switch their allegiances.

Although under the provisions of the City Code an offer may be declared unconditional when acceptances reach 50 per cent of the share capital, the normal condition of any offer is 90 per cent or such lower percentage in excess of 50 per cent as the offeror may decide. This is usually expressed as a 90 per cent condition which can be waived. The condition is expressed this way as it is only at the 90 per cent level that the provisions of sections 428 and 429 of the Companies Act 1985 can be invoked so as compulsorily to acquire the minority shareholders. In the case of an MBO these provisions have an added importance in that the lending banks will make it a condition of the banking arrangements that the offer not be declared unconditional until the acceptance level reaches 90 per cent. In practice the bank or banks may be prepared, in the event, to permit Newco to declare the offer unconditional at a lower level, say 75 per cent (see below), but only if, after careful enquiry and scrutiny, the investment banking adviser to Newco is able to give firm assurances that the 90 per cent level will in due course be met. There is certainly a chicken and egg situation here as many investors (e.g. index funds and hedge funds) may be unprepared to accept the offer until after it has been declared unconditional so a momentum has to be maintained, particularly if the offer is to be concluded within 42 days. The position may be exacerbated if significant trading has accrued during the offer period with shares ending up in the hands of arbitrageurs who will normally only accept the offer when the game is up and they are convinced that a better price cannot be obtained for their shares. Nonetheless, these arbitrageurs will probably have been trading on very tight margins or spreads over the cost of funds so that when the game is over they will accept very quickly. The imminent delisting of the target's shares from the Stock Exchange will also provide an incentive.

It may also be possible, in conjunction with the equity house, to have funds available to make market purchases of the target company's shares during the offer period so as to soak up some of the shares which become available on the market, thus avoiding the possibility of such shares falling into the hands of any third party who may wish to frustrate the offer. Under the Takeover Code, such purchases may only be made at prices at or below the offer price and care will be needed to ensure that the insider dealing provisions of the Financial Services Act are not breached.

The importance of the 75 per cent level of acceptances mentioned above is that, at this level, Newco will be able to pass a special resolution at a meeting of shareholders of the target company (including that for the privatization of the target company) and also under UK tax law the two companies will form a group for tax purposes. This will be important in order to obtain tax relief for the interest paid by Newco on the borrowings which it has raised to acquire the target company.

Once the offer has been declared unconditional the hard work will begin for the MBO team. The main issues will be to pay the shareholders in the target company for their shares by drawing down the facilities made available for the offer, then embarking upon the considerable task of running the business in accordance with the business plan and model and repaying the bank and other debt as quickly as possible. Most venture capitalists and equity houses would say that the success of an MBO deal over its life will depend critically upon the performance of the business over the first one to two years after the deal has been concluded. This point has already been made in Chapter 6 dealing with the preparation of the business plan and model.

FURTHER LEGAL AND TECHNICAL MATTERS

However, there will unfortunately continue to be further legal and technical matters to be attended to:

Acquiring minority shareholdings

Once the 90 per cent level of acceptances has been reached the section 429 provisions must be invoked to acquire the outstanding minority on the same terms as the offer – 'must', because this will have been a provision in the banking documentation. Under these provisions the shares held by the minority will become vested in Newco 42 days after the posting of notices to such shareholders unless such shareholders accept the offer in the intervening period.

The whitewash procedure

Once the section 429 procedure has been completed it will normally be necessary to go through the whitewash procedure. This is the name which has been colloquially given to the procedure under sections 155 to 157 of the Companies Act 1985 whereby a company, having first re-registered as a private limited company so as to take advantage of the provisions, is able to give financial assistance to its new parent company Newco. In practice this means that the banks can receive the assets of the target company as security for their loans and surplus cash generated out of 'pre-acquisition' profits. Giving financial assistance without complying with these provisions would amount to a criminal offence under the Act.

The first step is to re-register as a private limited company under sections 53 and 54 of the Act. This must be done by special resolution by amending the target company's memorandum of association. As long as the target is wholly owned this can be done on short notice and as a formality. If minority shareholders still remain then shareholders representing 5 per cent of the share capital can apply to the court within 28 days to have the resolution cancelled, although the court does not normally intervene in this way.

The second step is to go through the requirements and procedures of sections 155 to 157 to implement the whitewash. In broad terms these are as follows:

- that the memorandum and articles of the target company must give the company power to enter into the security arrangements and not prohibit the giving of financial assistance;

- that the net assets are not reduced by giving the financial assistance or, if so reduced, such reduction is covered by distributable reserves;

- that all directors make a statutory declaration of solvency complying with section 156;

- that the auditors to the target company report that the opinion expressed by the directors in the statutory declaration is not unreasonable in all the circumstances;

- that a special resolution of the target company must be passed approving the giving of the financial assistance. Holders of 10 per cent or more of the share capital of the target (in cases where the compulsory acquisition procedure has not been applied) can apply to the court within 28 days to cancel the resolution.

In practice, all the companies in the target group, i.e. the offeree company and all its subsidiaries, will be required to go through the whitewash procedure. This will necessitate board meetings and declarations in respect of all such companies.

FURTHER PROCEDURAL MATTERS

Further procedural matters which will need to be attended to include:

- the delisting of the target company's shares from the relevant stock exchange;

- the completion of the debenture documentation in favour of the banks so as to give the necessary security. This can only be done in respect of acquisition finance (other than in respect of the shares in the target company) once the whitewash procedure has been completed but can be given for working capital advances immediately;

- the setting up of the hedging arrangements (discussed in Chapter 5) required by the banks so as to limit Newco's exposure to interest rate increases;

- the payment of the fees in respect of the transaction. With investment bankers and lawyers on each side, accountants, valuers and other professionals together with upfront fees to the lending banks and the equity house, the fees may well amount to 5 to 6 per cent of the offer value. There will also be annual monitoring fees to the equity house and possibly the banks.

SUMMARY

It can be seen that the retention of a small minority shareholding can severely delay the giving of financial assistance which will be of concern to the banks. The minority will normally be a nuisance factor in these matters but it is far better to have been able to invoke the compulsory acquisition procedures and to go through these arrangements as a wholly owned subsidiary.

Finally, it is worth mentioning that the loan documentation will continually have to be monitored to ensure that all the provisions are being observed and the covenants met. There will be a requirement to give detailed and timely financial information to the banks on a monthly basis and this information will probably be much more detailed than the company will have prepared previously.

Taxation issues

INTRODUCTION

It is difficult to be specific on all the taxation issues which will affect a management buyout as these will vary from transaction to transaction. There are, nonetheless, some particular issues which will need specific attention when considering an MBO and these are dealt with in the sections below.

CAPITAL GAINS TAX

If management already have a reasonable level of investment in the target company and they are to make a significant investment in the MBO itself, then steps should be taken to see whether an immediate charge to capital gains tax can be avoided on the disposal of the shares in the target company. Management will usually be required to invest in a combination of shares and deferred loan notes in the MBO vehicle and it may be possible to arrange this so that the share for share exchange relief is available. In this case it may be necessary to obtain the approval of the Panel on Takeovers and Mergers as this is a benefit which will not be available to shareholders generally.

There may be a further benefit to be received from such a transaction in that taper relief (which replaced indexation) from capital gains tax may also be available on the investment in the MBO vehicle. Specialist advice will need to be taken on this as there has been press speculation that this has been denied on one or two high-profile transactions and the nature of the security held by the investor may be critical.

INHERITANCE TAX

Because management will be investing a relatively modest sum of money into a transaction where, if everything goes well, a very substantial investment could result, it may be possible to take steps at the outset to ensure that such value accrues outside the executive's estate, by, for example, making the initial investment through family trusts. This is an area where high-level specialist advice will be needed to ensure that any anti-avoidance provisions are not fallen foul of and to ensure that no immediate charge to tax arises, which will depend on the executive's specific circumstances.

RELIEF FOR INTEREST PAID

Being a highly leveraged transaction the MBO vehicle will have significant interest costs to pay, both to the financing banks and to the equity house. With no taxable profits of its own, tax relief will be obtainable, subject to what is said below, by setting the interest against the profits of the target company (i.e. the business) under the grouping provisions. This requires 75 per cent ownership of the target company but this will almost always be a precondition of the offer being declared unconditional.

The equity house will be looking for a significant return on its investment and as a large part of this will have been invested by way of a high interest-bearing subordinated loan, the equity house will look for as high an interest rate as possible on that loan, the balance of the equity house's return being by way of dividend on its straight equity investment. The Inland Revenue is likely to restrict the tax relief on interest to the equity house to that on a fair commercial rate of interest and, again, specialist advice will need to be taken as to what that might be in the specific circumstances of each case.

FEES PAID IN THE TRANSACTION – VAT AND TAX RELIEF

There will be very significant fees paid in arranging the transaction. These will fall under four general headings:

- *Costs of making the offer*. The main costs under this heading will be the fee payable to the investment bank for making the offer and the stamp duty payable on the transfer of the shares to Newco. It is unlikely that any of these costs will receive any tax relief.
- *Costs payable by the target*. These costs will include the costs payable by the target company to its investment banking (Rule 3) adviser and also to its lawyers. There may also be some costs payable to the company's auditors for verifying information for inclusion in the offer document. Again it is unlikely that these costs will rank for taxation relief.
- *Due diligence*. Significant costs will be incurred in the due diligence exercises outlined in Chapter 4. The largest fees will be payable to the lawyers and the investigating accountants but there may also be significant fees payable to others, for example for property valuation.
- *Bank fees*. The lending banks will almost certainly require the payment of significant arrangement fees as well as annual commitment fees on undrawn facilities. It should be possible for tax relief to be obtained on the latter in the normal way.

As far as the due diligence costs and arrangement fees to the banks are concerned, many, if not all, of these will normally be regarded as costs of obtaining the finance and, accordingly, will be amortized over the life of the loans. Tax relief should then be obtainable on a group relief basis in accordance with the accounting treatment. This again is a complex area on which further detailed advice should be obtained.

It is also vital that the invoices be rendered to the correct company to ensure the appropriate treatment.

As far as VAT is concerned, specialist advice should be obtained but relief will normally be available in respect of VAT paid on the transaction fees. It is important that Newco and the target company become part of the same VAT group registration before the fees are paid.

OTHER ISSUES

There may be other taxation issues which will need to be considered in particular cases and it is not possible to give a complete review here. For example, items which could be relevant in certain instances are the following:

■ If the target company is a member of a larger group, corporation tax on capital gains liabilities could arise in respect of previous intra-group transfers as a result of leaving the group. While this is more likely on the trade sale of a wholly owned subsidiary it could apply where a listed company is itself a 75 per cent subsidiary of a larger group.

■ If the target company has accrued any unrelieved trading losses for tax purposes, care will need to be taken that the anti-avoidance provisions, which can cause such tax losses to be forfeited, are not fallen foul of. These apply where, over a three-year period, there has been a change of ownership and also a significant change in the nature or scale of the operations of the company.

There will be specific issues to be considered in each individual case on which the company's advisers' opinions must be sought.

Exit strategies

DEFINITION

Reference has been made on several occasions to the fact that the equity house will need to realize its investment over a limited period of time. This is known colloquially in the industry as 'the exit'. The requirement for the exit stems from the fact that the equity house itself is normally a financial investor and, furthermore, it will often have raised pools of funds from investors with an indication of the period over which the investments made with such funds will be realized. Both the equity house and the investors will have target rates of return which they hope to realize from the investments made.

FLOTATION

If the business performs according to or better than the business plan and model agreed at the outset, it is likely that the business will be in a suitable shape to be floated or refloated on the Stock Exchange. The combination of a strong growth in profits together with a build up in the net worth of the business through the retention of earnings will give rise to a healthy business, which in turn should attract portfolio investors. Management's stake in the business will, in these circumstances, have increased as a result of the ratchet mechanism, giving them the performance-related reward of further equity. Although the equity house would normally dispose of its whole investment, sometimes it will be prepared to retain a significant stake in the newly listed company. Also, if there is a need for further equity capital in the business at the time of listing it will often be possible for the company to issue new shares.

While this scenario is very satisfactory from everyone's point of view and will be the normal form of exit for the equity house, management may consider that the listing puts them back to the same position that they were in before the MBO itself, i.e. running a listed company which may still be too small to attract long-term institutional support from investors so that after a period of time it once again becomes undervalued and orphaned by investors. There are nonetheless two very important differences which make the journey worthwhile:

- Management will have secured the future of the business and their involvement and employment in it for a further period of time with a limited capital commitment on their part.

- Management will have amassed a significant shareholding in the company which may be realized over a period of time or be provided as a platform for an offer by a third party for the company.

Whatever the outcome, if the forecasts in the business model have been met, management are likely to be far wealthier than they may perhaps even have thought possible.

TRADE SALE

In the event that the performance of the business falls significantly short of that predicted by the business plan and model, the flotation of the business is unlikely to be a viable proposition. In these circumstances, it may well be that the equity house will continue to own most of the share capital of the business as the ratchet which gives the performance-related equity to management will either not have been triggered or will only have given rise to a small increase in the management equity. The equity house will then look for a different exit and this will often be by way of a trade sale to an existing company operating in the same field. The proceeds to the equity house will normally be less in these circumstances due to several factors:

- the poor trading performance;
- a likely high level of residual debt;
- the lack of a stock exchange valuation from which negotiations can take place.

Management will normally, in the event of the trade sale, realize whatever investment they have in the business and may also cease to be employed within the business unless the new owners wish or require them to remain. Management may not regard this as a very satisfactory outcome but their stay with the company may still have been longer than it would otherwise have been if they had not initiated the MBO and thus remained open to the vagaries of the market. They may also take some satisfaction from the fact that they attempted the transaction and any failure may have been from unforeseen extraneous factors. In any event, unless the business has utterly failed, it is likely that they will have made a reasonable amount of money even if not 'becoming rich beyond the dreams of avarice'.

RECAPITALIZATION

A less conventional way in which the equity house may obtain its exit is from the cash flow of the business itself. This can only arise in the case of a business with very strong profits growth and high margins as not only will the business have to provide sufficient cash to pay the interest and dividends to the banks and equity investor but it will also have to repay the larger part of the bank debt and the initial investment of the equity investor, most of which will have been provided by way of subordinated debt. Even if this can be done, the equity investor will normally have a residual stake in the business after management has triggered the ratchet and it may be necessary for the business to embark upon a secondary buyout or recapitalization to acquire this resultant stake and take the business into 100 per cent control. Transactions of this nature are not commonplace due largely to the financial criteria required but also due to the strains which will be put upon the business. In some cases this may result in a reduction in the scale of the business as it uses its cash generation to meet the financial obligations. If this form of exit can be produced it can be highly attractive to management as it means that with 100 per cent control the business has been taken private and can be kept private until management decide to sell out completely to either a trade buyer or by flotation. A further variant on this would be to structure the management ownership in the form of a trust, although the equity house will require there to be sufficient flexibility to ensure that it can realize its investment if the business does not perform to plan.

As the market for initial public offerings or flotations has weakened, greater emphasis has been placed upon the recapitalization or secondary buyout. If this is pursued the finance may be obtained either from bank financing if the business is strong enough to support this further debt or from another equity house which may be prepared to provide the initial financiers with their exit and take a robust view of the business and its prospects for the next stage in its development.

SUMMARY

While the transactions outlined in this chapter do not form part of the MBO process at inception, it is important that management understand before they embark upon the transaction what the ultimate ownership of the business is likely to be and what options are open to them. If management's main objective is with making a significant capital profit then they may be less concerned with which exit route is ultimately chosen. However, most management teams do have an affection and affinity with the business despite the vicissitudes of business life.

Conclusion

SUCCESSFUL CONCLUSION

It may have occurred to the reader of this book that to embark upon an MBO, let alone see it through and then operate the business for the ensuing few years so as to pay down the debt and repay the equity house, is a mammoth uphill task. So it may be, but the potential rewards can be enormous. Furthermore, as in many walks of life, the timing and nature of the encashment of any reward may be very different from those anticipated. For example, business may boom and stock market conditions be ripe for an early flotation or the opportunity may arise in such circumstances for a trade sale. Much will depend upon the objectives, needs and lifestyle requirements of the management team. In some cases there may be a desire to acquire the target company and keep it private, out of the public gaze. In others, management may not bother as long as a significant profit can be made on the way through. Certainly, an *ésprit de corps* and the attainment of a common goal should bring the management team closer together in seeing the MBO to a conclusion.

NEED OF SUPPORT

What, though, if things go wrong and the business plan and model cannot be met? This will usually be because a sound business has been burdened with a large amount of debt and business has turned down in the early stages of the life of the MBO. As long as it is the economy and the industry which give rise to this difficulty rather than the business itself, there is every chance that the banks and, in particular, the equity house will be supportive. After all, neither will wish to run the business themselves and they will be reluctant to find other management to do so. In these circumstances they will probably instigate some form of restructuring in which further cash is injected or loan terms renegotiated to take the business through a difficult patch. Of course, they will not support a lost cause or continue to support a management team which has lost its way and in such circumstances would take their losses. If a restructuring does take place, then this will probably involve management reducing its equity stake either by dilution from the issue of further shares or by foregoing some or all of the benefits of the ratchet which may be unattainable in any event by this stage. However, if the management still have their jobs and a piece of the action, then all will not be lost and at least they will be able to say that they 'had a go', something they might otherwise regret for the rest of their lives.

REFLECTING ON THE DEAL

Management should also not lose sight of the reasons why they embarked upon the buyout in the first place. They will have done so either because they saw an opportunity or because the business was undervalued by the market or going through a difficult trading patch, either of which put the company at risk from the predatory inclinations of competitors or other financial buyers. Sometimes both reasons may have been factors in their action. To companies in these situations, the future is in any event uncertain and by taking the pre-emptive action the management team will have limited the external risk to the period of the offer. If they come through this they will have secured their gainful employment for the future in a quasi-proprietorial role. They will obviously have to continue to come up to the mark in their performance and the high levels of debt imposed on the business in the early stages will increase the risks of failure, but the support of a strong equity house will normally see the business through any difficult period. At the end of the day, a more focused, efficient and profitable business will hopefully emerge from the sheer discipline of the exercise and the entrepreneurial spirit which has been released.

Appendices

Outline timetable

D – 120   Management concludes that it wishes to formally consider an MBO and splits the board for this purpose. Non-executive directors appoint a Rule 3 adviser.

D – 100   General agreement on terms and consent received from non-executive directors to commence due diligence.

D – 42   Final work on model commenced.
Final rounds of negotiations with banks.
Final rounds of negotiations with equity house. Negotiation and drafting of legal agreements and bank documentation.
Drafting of offer document.

D – 3   Signing of legal agreements and bank facility agreement.
Obtaining of irrevocable undertakings.

D – 2   Formal announcement of offer for target company to Stock Exchange.

DAY 0   Posting of offer document to target company shareholders.

D + 21   First closing date of offer.

D + 42   Offer declared unconditional (assumed date).

D + 50   Acceptances reach 90 per cent – despatch section 429 notices to acquire compulsorily minority (assumed date).

D + 52   Debentures executed over target company shares and over target assets (the latter for working capital only).

D + 56   First payments to accepting shareholders.

D + 60   Final date on which offer may be declared unconditional or otherwise lapses.

D + 92   Minority acquired under section 429 procedure taking ownership to 100 per cent.

D + 100   Meetings held to pass whitewash resolutions in order to give financial assistance following which debenture may be executed over target company's assets for all facilities.

UBS Warburg Business Plan and Model

Mgmt

Sources of Funds

Sources of Funds	GBP m	%	Margin	Rate	Tenor	Av. Life
Drawn Revolver			2.25%	8.74%	7.0 years	-
Term loan A			2.25%	8.74%	7.0 years	-
Term loan B			2.75%	9.24%	8.0 years	-
Term loan C			3.25%	9.74%	8.5 years	-
Term loan D			3.75%	10.24%	9.0 years	-
Senior debt	-	-				-
Mezzanine			3.50%	9.99%	10.0 years	-
High Yield			6.36%	12.00%	10.0 years	-
Subordinated debt	-	-				-
Total debt	-	-				-
Shareholder Loan Note				10.00%		-
Ordinary Equity + Prefs			-	-	-	-
Total Equity	-	-				-
Total sources	-	-				-

Interest Rate - Base	GBP m	%	2.25%	8.74%	7.0 years	
Revolver			2.25%	8.74%	7.0 years	
				6.49%		

Uses of Funds	GBP m	%		Share Price/Bid Value	
Purchase of equity				Current Price	-
Refinance existing debt				Offer Price	-
Excess cash				No.Shares (m)	-
Repay prefs				Option Cost	-
Fees and expenses				Equity Bid	-
Total uses	-	-		Premium	-

MODEL ASSUMPTIONS

Selected Scenario	Mgnt ►
CCY (e.g. EUR mm)	GBP m

Disposals?	☐

Goodwill	
Deductible?	☐
Tax Deductibility	0.0%
Amortisation	20 Years

Fees and Expenses	
Deductible?	☐
Tax Deductibility	0.0%
Amortisation	10 Years
RCF Commitment Fee	0.75%

Corporate Tax Rate	30.0%
EBITDA Exit Multiple	0.00 x
Fixed Charge Cover	1.20 x

Mezzanine	
Full Cash Pay?	☐
PIK Interest	0.0%
Cash Interest After...	4 Years
Redemption Premium	0.0%

High Yield	
Cash Pay?	☑
Cash Interest After...	6 Years
Redemption Premium	0.0%

Shareholder Loan Note	
Full coupon PIK?	☑
Convert to ordinary equity on exit?	0.0%
Cash Interest from Year...	2002
PIK Tax Deductibility	50.0%

Management Options	Free ►
Next Business year end	30-Sep-01
Acquiring date	01-Mar-01

PURCHASE PRICE MULTIPLE (ex. fees & cash)

	2000	2001	2002
Sales	0.00x	0.00x	0.00x
EBITDA	0.00x	0.00x	0.00x
EBITA	0.00x	0.00x	0.00x

IRR Calculations for Financial Sponsor

	2003	2004	2005
EBITDA	Exit	**Exit**	Exit
Multiple			
-0.50 x	-	-	-
0.00 x	-	-	-
0.50 x	-	-	-

IRR Calculations for Mezzanine Investor

	2004	
EBITDA	Exit	
Multiple		
-0.50 x	-	
0.00 x	-	
0.50 x	-	

SUMMARY FINANCIAL RESULTS

Y/E 30-Sep	1997	1998	1999	2000 30-Sep-00	2001 5.0 months	Pro Forma	2001 7.0 months	2001 12 months	2002	2003	2004	2005	2006	2007	2008	2009	2010
Sales							0.6	-	1.6	2.6	3.6	4.6	5.6	6.6	7.6	8.6	9.6
% growth																	
% CAGR (base 2000)																	
EBITDA																	
EBITDA margin																	
EBITA																	
EBITA margin																	
Capital expenditures																	
Capex / Depreciation																	
Total interest expenses																	
Total cash interest expenses																	
Senior cash interest expenses																	
Tax payment in cash																	
Working capital inflow / (outflow)																	
Operating cash flow																	
Cash																	
Revolver																	
Term loan A																	
Term loan B																	
Term loan C																	
Term loan D																	
Mezzanine																	
High Yield																	
Total debt																	
Total net debt																	
Total senior debt																	
Total senior net debt																	
Total equity (inc. shareholder notes)																	
Total capitalisation																	

SUMMARY CREDIT STATISTICS

Y/E 30-Sep	Pro Forma 30-Sep-00	LTM 30-Nov-00	LTM 31-Jan-01	LTM 28-Feb-01	Pro Forma 2001	2002	2003	2004	2005	2006	2007	2008	2009	2010
EBITA / Senior cash interest expense														
EBITA / Total cash interest expense														
EBITA / Total interest expense														
EBITDA / Senior cash interest expense														
EBITDA / Total cash interest expense														
EBITDA / Total interest expense														
EBITDA - capex / Total cash interest expense														
Senior debt / EBITDA														
Total debt / EBITDA														
Total net debt / EBITDA														
Senior fixed charge cover														
Total fixed charge cover														
Total net debt / Total capitalisation														

Strictly Confidential

PROJECT ***** - Mgmt Case
PRO-FORMA BALANCE SHEET

Mgmt

| | Y/E 30-Sep | | | | Closing | Adjustments | | PF Opening |
	1997	1998	1999	2000	28-Feb-01	Debit	Credit	1-Mar-01
Cash and cash equivalents	-	-	-	-	-	-	-	-
Debtors and prepayments	-	-	-	-	-	-	-	-
Other debtors	-	-	-	-	-	-	-	-
Inventory	-	-	-	-	-	-	-	-
Other current assets	-	-	-	-	-	-	-	-
Current asset add-back	-	-	-	-	-	-	-	-
Total current assets	-	-	-	-	-			-
Gross fixed assets	-	-	-	-	-	-	-	-
Accumulated depreciation	-	-	-	-	-	-	-	-
Net fixed assets	-	-	-	-	-			-
Other long-term assets	-	-	-	-	-	-	-	-
Accumulated amortisation	-	-	-	-	-	-	-	-
Capitalized fees & expenses	-	-	-	-	-	-	-	-
Goodwill	-	-	-	-	-	-	-	-
Total assets	-	-	-	-	-			-
Accounts payable	-	-	-	-	-	-	-	-
Accrued liabilities	-	-	-	-	-	-	-	-
Suppliers of fixed assets	-	-	-	-	-	-	-	-
Other current liabilities	-	-	-	-	-	-	-	-
Total current liabilities	-	-	-	-	-			-
Revolver	-	-	-	-	-	-	-	-
Term loan A	-	-	-	-	-	-	-	-
Term loan B	-	-	-	-	-	-	-	-
Term loan C	-	-	-	-	-	-	-	-
Term loan D	-	-	-	-	-	-	-	-
Mezzanine	-	-	-	-	-	-	-	-
High Yield	-	-	-	-	-	-	-	-
Total debt	-	-	-	-	-			-
Deferred taxes	-	-	-	-	-	-	-	-
Pension liabilities	-	-	-	-	-	-	-	-
Risk reserves and provisions	-	-	-	-	-	-	-	-
Other long-term liabilities	-	-	-	-	-	-	-	-
Total liabilities	-	-	-	-	-			-
Shareholder Loan Note	-	-	-	-	-	-	-	-
Common equity	-	-	-	-	-	-	-	-
Retained earnings	-	-	-	-	-	-	-	-
Total equity	-	-	-	-	-			-
Total liabilities & equity	-	-	-	-	-	-		-
	OK	OK	OK	OK	OK	OK	OK	OK

CONSOLIDATED
PROJECT *** - Mgmt Case**
PROFIT & LOSS ACCOUNT

Mgm

Strictly Confidential

	1997	Y/E 30-Sep 1998	1999	2000	5.0 months 2001	7.0 months 2001	12 months 2001	2002	2003	2004	Y/E 30-Sep 2005	2006	2007	2008	2009	2010
Net Sales																
Other Revenue																
Total Revenue																
Variable COS																
Other Variable COS																
Gross profit																
General Fixed COS																
Other Personnel costs																
Other Sales & Marketing																
Contingencies																
Other Income / (Costs)																
Adjustment - Cost Reduction Programme																
EBITDA																
Depreciation - Fixed Assets																
EBITA																
Amortisation - Intangible Assets																
Amortisation of goodwill																
Amortisation of fees																
Operating EBIT																
Exceptional income / (costs)																
Reorganisation Costs																
Profit / (loss) on disposal																
EBIT after nonrec.																
Interest expenses (inc. non-cash)																
Interest income																
Extraordinaries (cash)																
Risk reserves and provisions (non-cash)																
EBT																
Tax - Current																
- Deferred																
Net income																
Preferred dividends (PIK)																
Net income after preferred dividends																
Dividends on common																
INCOME STATEMENT RATIOS																
Sales growth																
Gross profit margin																
EBITDA margin																
EBITA margin																
EBIT margin																

CONSOLIDATED
PROJECT ***** - Mgmt Case
BALANCE SHEET

Mgmt

	1997	Y/E 30-Sep 1998	1999	2000	Closing 28-Feb-01	Opening 1-Mar-01	2001	2002	2003	2004	Y/E 30-Sep 2005	2006	2007	2008	2009	2010
Cash and cash equivalents																
Debtors and prepayments																
Other debtors																
Inventory																
Other current assets																
Current asset add-back																
Total current assets																
Gross fixed assets																
Accumulated depreciation																
Net fixed assets																
Other long-term assets																
Accumulated amortisation																
Capitalized fees & expenses																
Goodwill																
Total assets																
Accounts payable																
Accrued liabilities																
Suppliers of fixed assets																
Other current liabilities																
Total current liabilities																
Revolver																
Term loan A																
Term loan B																
Term loan C																
Term loan D																
Mezzanine																
High Yield																
Total debt																
Deferred taxes																
Pension liabilities																
Risk reserves and provisions																
Other long-term liabilities																
Total liabilities																
Shareholder Loan Note																
Common equity																
Retained earnings																
Total equity																
Total liabilities & equity																
	OK	OK	OK	OK	OK	OK	OK	OK	OK	OK	OK	OK	OK	OK	OK	OK

UBS Warburg

CONSOLIDATED
PROJECT *** - Mgmt Case**
CASH FLOW STATEMENT

Mgmt

	1997	Y/E 30-Sep 1998	1999	2000	5.0 months 2001	7.0 months 2001	2002	2003	2004	Y/E 30-Sep 2005	2006	2007	2008	2009	2010
CASH FLOW FROM OPERATING ACTIVITIES															
Operating EBIT															
Exceptional income / (costs)															
Reorganisation Costs															
EBIT after nonrec.															
Plus:															
Depreciation - Fixed Assets															
Amortisation - Intangible Assets															
Amortisation of goodwill															
Amortisation of fees															
EBITDA (post reorganisaton costs)															
Less:															
Current taxes															
Change in working capital:															
Debtors and prepayments															
Other debtors															
Inventory															
Other current assets															
Accounts payable															
Accrued liabilities															
Other current liabilities															
Current asset add-back on disposal															
Total change in working capital															
Change in other long-term assets															
Change in liabilities to suppliers of fixed assets															
Change in pension liabilities															
Change in other long-term liabilities															
Extraordinary items (cash)															
Net cash flow from operating activities															
CASH FLOW FROM INVESTING ACTIVITIES															
Capital expenditures															
Asset sales proceeds															
Net cash from (used in) investing activities															
OPERATING CASH FLOW															
CASH FLOW FROM FINANCING ACTIVITIES															
Interest Expenses															
Interest Income															
Increase (decrease) in Revolver															
Increase (decrease) in Term Loan A															
Increase (decrease) in Term Loan B															
Increase (decrease) in Term Loan C															
Increase (decrease) in Term Loan D															
Increase (decrease) in Mezzanine															
Increase (decrease) in High Yield															
Increase (decrease) in Shareholder Loan Note															
Increase (decrease) in Common Equity															
Dividend on common															
Net cash from (used in) financing activities															
NET CASH FLOW															
Cash balance (BF)															
Cash surplus															
Cash balance (CF)															

CONSOLIDATED
PROJECT ***** - Mgmt Case
DEBT SCHEDULE

Mgmt

	Pro Forma 2001	7.0 months 0.59 2001	1.59 2002	2.59 2003	3.59 2004	Y/E 30-Sep 4.59 2005	5.59 2006	6.59 2007	7.59 2008	8.59 2009	9.59 2010
Cash flow from operating activities		-	-	-	-	-	-	-	-	-	-
less: capital expenditure		-	-	-	-	-	-	-	-	-	-
plus: proceeds from asset sales		-	-	-	-	-	-	-	-	-	-
less: dividend on common		-	-	-	-	-	-	-	-	-	-
Minimum cash balance		-	-	-	-	-	-	-	-	-	-
Cash buffer		-	-	-	-	-	-	-	-	-	-
Cash Interest Expense		-	-	-	-	-	-	-	-	-	-
Free Cash Flow (Cash available for debt repayment)		-	-	-	-	-	-	-	-	-	-
Cash flow before cash buffer		-	-	-	-	-	-	-	-	-	-
Simple cash buffer		-	-	-	-	-	-	-	-	-	-
Cash flow after simple cash buffer		-	-	-	-	-	-	-	-	-	-
Cash buffer		-	-	-	-	-	-	-	-	-	-

Target Minimum 1.20 16.7%

Term loan A

	Pro Forma 2001	2001	2002	2003	2004	2005	2006	2007	2008	2009	2010
Beginning Balance		-	-	-	-	-	-	-	-	-	-
Scheduled Amortization		-	-	-	-	-	-	-	-	-	-
Prepayment		-	-	-	-	-	-	-	-	-	-
Ending Balance	-	-	-	-	-	-	-	-	-	-	-
Interest Rate @ 8.74%		8.7%	8.7%	8.7%	8.7%	8.7%	8.7%	8.7%	8.7%	8.7%	8.7%
Interest Expense		-	-	-	-	-	-	-	-	-	-

Prepay ? yes

CF available post scheduled amortization of term loan A

Term loan B

	Pro Forma 2001	2001	2002	2003	2004	2005	2006	2007	2008	2009	2010
Beginning Balance		-	-	-	-	-	-	-	-	-	-
Scheduled Amortization		-	-	-	-	-	-	-	-	-	-
Prepayment		-	-	-	-	-	-	-	-	-	-
Ending Balance	-	-	-	-	-	-	-	-	-	-	-
Interest Rate @ 9.24%		9.2%	9.2%	9.2%	9.2%	9.2%	9.2%	9.2%	9.2%	9.2%	9.2%
Interest Expense		-	-	-	-	-	-	-	-	-	-

Prepay ? yes

CF available post scheduled amortization of term loan B

Term loan C

	Pro Forma 2001	2001	2002	2003	2004	2005	2006	2007	2008	2009	2010
Beginning Balance		-	-	-	-	-	-	-	-	-	-
Scheduled Amortization		-	-	-	-	-	-	-	-	-	-
Prepayment		-	-	-	-	-	-	-	-	-	-
Ending Balance	-	-	-	-	-	-	-	-	-	-	-
Interest Rate @ 9.74%		9.7%	9.7%	9.7%	9.7%	9.7%	9.7%	9.7%	9.7%	9.7%	9.7%
Interest Expense		-	-	-	-	-	-	-	-	-	-

Prepay ? yes

CF available post scheduled amortization of term loan C

Term Loan D

	Pro Forma 2001	2001	2002	2003	2004	2005	2006	2007	2008	2009	2010
Beginning Balance		-	-	-	-	-	-	-	-	-	-
Scheduled Amortization		-	-	-	-	-	-	-	-	-	-
Prepayment		-	-	-	-	-	-	-	-	-	-
Ending Balance	-	-	-	-	-	-	-	-	-	-	-
Interest Rate @ 10.24%		10.2%	10.2%	10.2%	10.2%	10.2%	10.2%	10.2%	10.2%	10.2%	10.2%
Interest Expense		-	-	-	-	-	-	-	-	-	-

Prepay ? yes

CF available post scheduled amortization of term loan D

CONSOLIDATED
PROJECT *** - Mgmt Case**
DEBT SCHEDULE

Mgmt

	Pro Forma 2001	0.59 / 7.0 months 2001	1.59 2002	2.59 2003	3.59 2004	4.59 Y/E 30-Sep 2005	5.59 2006	6.59 2007	7.59 2008	8.59 2009	9.59 2010
Mezzanine											
Beginning Balance		-	-	-	-	-	-	-	-	-	-
Scheduled Amortization		-	-	-	-	-	-	-	-	-	-
Prepayment [Prepay ? no]		-	-	-	-	-	-	-	-	-	-
Full interest in cash ?		no	no	no	no	yes	yes	yes	yes	yes	yes
Capitalization of interest [0.0%]		-	-	-	-	-	-	-	-	-	-
Ending Balance	-	-	-	-	-	-	-	-	-	-	-
Interest Rate @ 9.99%		10.0%	10.0%	10.0%	10.0%	10.0%	10.0%	10.0%	10.0%	10.0%	10.0%
Interest Expense (incl. capitalization)		-	-	-	-	-	-	-	-	-	-

CF available post scheduled amortization of Mezzanine

High Yield											
Beginning Balance		-	-	-	-	-	-	-	-	-	-
Scheduled Amortization		-	-	-	-	-	-	-	-	-	-
Prepayment [Prepay ? no]		-	-	-	-	-	-	-	-	-	-
Interest in cash ?		yes	yes	yes	yes	yes	yes	yes	yes	yes	yes
Capitalization of interest [12.0%]		-	-	-	-	-	-	-	-	-	-
Ending Balance	-	-	-	-	-	-	-	-	-	-	-
Interest Rate @ 12.00%		12.0%	12.0%	12.0%	12.0%	12.0%	12.0%	12.0%	12.0%	12.0%	12.0%
Interest Expense (incl. capitalization)		-	-	-	-	-	-	-	-	-	-

CF available post scheduled amortization of High Yield

Shareholder Loan Note											
Beginning Balance		-	-	-	-	-	-	-	-	-	-
Scheduled Amortization		-	-	-	-	-	-	-	-	-	-
Prepayment [Prepay ? no]		-	-	-	-	-	-	-	-	-	-
Interest in cash ?		no	no	no	no	no	no	no	no	no	no
Capitalization of interest [10.0%]		-	-	-	-	-	-	-	-	-	-
Ending Balance	-	-	-	-	-	-	-	-	-	-	-
Cash Interest Rate @ 0.00%		0.0%	0.0%	0.0%	0.0%	0.0%	0.0%	0.0%	0.0%	0.0%	0.0%
Interest Expense (incl. capitalization)		-	-	-	-	-	-	-	-	-	-

CF available post scheduled amortization of Shareholder Loan Note

CF available post scheduled amortizations and voluntary prepayment of R/C
CF available post scheduled amortizations and voluntary prepayment of R/C and TL A
CF available post scheduled amortizations and voluntary prepayment of R/C, TL A and B
CF available post scheduled amortizations and voluntary prepayment of R/C, TL A, B and C
CF available post scheduled amortizations and voluntary prepayment of R/C, TL A, B, C and D
CF available post sched. amort. and voluntary prep. of R/C, TL A, B & C, Term Loan D, Mezzanine
CF available post sched. amort. and voluntary prep. of R/C, TL A, B & C, Term Loan D, Mezzanine, High Yield
CF available post sched. amort. and voluntary prep. of R/C, TL A, B & C, Term Loan D, Mezzanine, High Yield, Shareholder Loan

Revolving credit											
Facility amount	-										
Beginning balance outstanding		-	-	-	-	-	-	-	-	-	-
Drawdown/(Repay) [Prepay ? no]	-										
Ending balance	-										
Assumed utilisation of revolver [25.0%]		-	-	-	-	-	-	-	-	-	-
Interest Rate @ 8.74%		8.7%	8.7%	8.7%	8.7%	8.7%	8.7%	8.7%	8.7%	8.7%	8.7%
Interest expense		-	-	-	-	-	-	-	-	-	-
Commitment Fee [0.75%]		-	-	-	-	-	-	-	-	-	-

CF available post all scheduled and voluntary prepayments (= Excess cash)

CONSOLIDATED
PROJECT *** - Mgmt Case**
DEBT SCHEDULE

Strictly Confidential

	Pro Forma 2001	0.59 7.0 months 2001	1.59 2002	2.59 2003	3.59 2004	4.59 Y/E 30-Sep 2005	5.59 2006	6.59 2007	7.59 2008	8.59 2009	9.59 2010
Seasonal debt											
Average seasonal debt in % of sales		0.0%	0.0%	0.0%	0.0%	0.0%	0.0%	0.0%	0.0%	0.0%	0.0%
Average seasonal debt		-	-	-	-	-	-	-	-	-	-
Interest rate on seasonal debt		8.7%	8.7%	8.7%	8.7%	8.7%	8.7%	8.7%	8.7%	8.7%	8.7%
Interest expense		-	-	-	-	-	-	-	-	-	-
Pension Liabilities											
Beginning Balance		-	-	-	-	-	-	-	-	-	-
Scheduled Amortization		-	-	-	-	-	-	-	-	-	-
Prepayment		-	-	-	-	-	-	-	-	-	-
Ending Balance	-	-	-	-	-	-	-	-	-	-	-
Interest Rate @ 0.00%	0.00%										
Interest Expense		0.0%	0.0%	0.0%	0.0%	0.0%	0.0%	0.0%	0.0%	0.0%	0.0%
		-	-	-	-	-	-	-	-	-	-
Debt summary											
Revolver	-	-	-	-	-	-	-	-	-	-	-
Term loan A	-	-	-	-	-	-	-	-	-	-	-
Term loan B	-	-	-	-	-	-	-	-	-	-	-
Term loan C	-	-	-	-	-	-	-	-	-	-	-
Term Loan D	-	-	-	-	-	-	-	-	-	-	-
Mezzanine	-	-	-	-	-	-	-	-	-	-	-
High Yield	-	-	-	-	-	-	-	-	-	-	-
Shareholder Loan Note	-	-	-	-	-	-	-	-	-	-	-
Total debt	-	-	-	-	-	-	-	-	-	-	-
Total interest expense summary											
Revolver	-	-	-	-	-	-	-	-	-	-	-
Term loan A	-	-	-	-	-	-	-	-	-	-	-
Term loan B	-	-	-	-	-	-	-	-	-	-	-
Term loan C	-	-	-	-	-	-	-	-	-	-	-
Term Loan D	-	-	-	-	-	-	-	-	-	-	-
Mezzanine	-	-	-	-	-	-	-	-	-	-	-
High Yield	-	-	-	-	-	-	-	-	-	-	-
Shareholder Loan Note	-	-	-	-	-	-	-	-	-	-	-
Seasonal debt	-	-	-	-	-	-	-	-	-	-	-
Pension Liabilities	-	-	-	-	-	-	-	-	-	-	-
Commitment fee on revolver	-	-	-	-	-	-	-	-	-	-	-
Total interest expense	-	-	-	-	-	-	-	-	-	-	-
Cash interest expense summary											
Revolver	-	-	-	-	-	-	-	-	-	-	-
Term loan A	-	-	-	-	-	-	-	-	-	-	-
Term loan B	-	-	-	-	-	-	-	-	-	-	-
Term loan C	-	-	-	-	-	-	-	-	-	-	-
Term loan D	-	-	-	-	-	-	-	-	-	-	-
Mezzanine	-	-	-	-	-	-	-	-	-	-	-
High Yield	-	-	-	-	-	-	-	-	-	-	-
Shareholder Loan Note	-	-	-	-	-	-	-	-	-	-	-
Seasonal debt	-	-	-	-	-	-	-	-	-	-	-
Pension Liabilities	-	-	-	-	-	-	-	-	-	-	-
Commitment fee on revolver	-	-	-	-	-	-	-	-	-	-	-
Total interest expense	-	-	-	-	-	-	-	-	-	-	-

Strictly Confidential

CONSOLIDATED
PROJECT *** - Mgmt Case**
EQUITY RETURNS

EQUITY OWNERSHIP

	Shareholder Loan	% Ownership	Common Investment	% Common Ownership	Warrants	Pre-Option Ownership	Perf. Options	Fully-Diluted
Investor 1	-	0.0%	-	#DIV/0!	0.0%	#DIV/0!	0.0%	#DIV/0!
Investor 2	-	0.0%	-	#DIV/0!	0.0%	#DIV/0!	0.0%	#DIV/0!
Investor 3	-	0.0%	-	#DIV/0!	0.0%	#DIV/0!	0.0%	#DIV/0!
Management	-	0.0%	-	#DIV/0!	0.0%	#DIV/0!	0.0%	#DIV/0!
Mezzanine	-	0.0%	-	0.0%	0.0%	0.0%	0.0%	0.0%
Total	**-**	**0.0%**	**-**	**#DIV/0!**	**0.0%**	**#DIV/0!**	**0.0%**	**#DIV/0!**

MANAGEMENT OPTIONS

No strike price included in net debt calculation

EXIT VALUE BASED ON EBITDA MULTIPLES

	EBITDA	Exit Multiple	Enterprise Value	Adjusted Net Debt	Shareholder Loan	Common Equity Value	Return Multiple	Investment Gain	IRR	Initial Investment	Year 0.6 2001	Year 1.6 2002	Year 2.6 2003	Year 3.6 2004	Year 4.6 2005
Investor 1 Return															
Year 5 Exit (2005)	-	(0.50) x	-	-	-	-	#DIV/0!	#DIV/0!	0.0%	-	#DIV/0!	#DIV/0!	#DIV/0!	#DIV/0!	#DIV/0!
	-	0.00 x	-	-	-	-	#DIV/0!	#DIV/0!	0.0%	-	#DIV/0!	#DIV/0!	#DIV/0!	#DIV/0!	#DIV/0!
	-	0.50 x	-	-	-	-	#DIV/0!	#DIV/0!	0.0%	-	#DIV/0!	#DIV/0!	#DIV/0!	#DIV/0!	#DIV/0!
Investor 1 Return															
Year 4 Exit (2004)	-	(0.50) x	-	-	-	-	#DIV/0!	#DIV/0!	0.0%	-	#DIV/0!	#DIV/0!	#DIV/0!	#DIV/0!	
	-	0.00 x	-	-	-	-	#DIV/0!	#DIV/0!	0.0%	-	#DIV/0!	#DIV/0!	#DIV/0!	#DIV/0!	
	-	0.50 x	-	-	-	-	#DIV/0!	#DIV/0!	0.0%	-	#DIV/0!	#DIV/0!	#DIV/0!	#DIV/0!	
Investor 1 Return															
Year 3 Exit (2003)	-	(0.50) x	-	-	-	-	#DIV/0!	#DIV/0!	0.0%	-	#DIV/0!	#DIV/0!	#DIV/0!		
	-	0.00 x	-	-	-	-	#DIV/0!	#DIV/0!	0.0%	-	#DIV/0!	#DIV/0!	#DIV/0!		
	-	0.50 x	-	-	-	-	#DIV/0!	#DIV/0!	0.0%	-	#DIV/0!	#DIV/0!	#DIV/0!		
Mezzanine										Mezzanine Debt and 0% Common					
Year 4 Exit (2004)	-	(0.50) x	-	-	-	-	0.00 x	0.0	0.0%	-	-	-	-	-	
	-	0.00 x	-	-	-	-	0.00 x	0.0	0.0%	-	-	-	-	-	
	-	0.50 x	-	-	-	-	0.00 x	0.0	0.0%	-	-	-	-	-	

Strictly Confidential

CONSOLIDATED
PROJECT ***** - Mgmt Case
MODEL ASSUMPTIONS

Mgmt

	Y/E 30-Sep								Y/E 30-Sep					
	1997	1998	1999	2000	2001	2002	2003	2004	2005	2006	2007	2008	2009	2010
SELECTED SCENARIO - Mgmt														
Sales Growth - Consolidated	-	-	-	-	-	-	-	-	-	-	-	-	-	-
Other Revenue	-	-	-	-	-	-	-	-	-	-	-	-	-	-
Variable COS (% Sales)	-	-	-	-	-	-	-	-	-	-	-	-	-	-
Other Variable COS (% total revenue)	-	-	-	-	-	-	-	-	-	-	-	-	-	-
General Fixed COS (% of total revenue)	-	-	-	-	-	-	-	-	-	-	-	-	-	-
Other Personnel (% of total revenue)	-	-	-	-	-	-	-	-	-	-	-	-	-	-
Other Sales & Marketing - % Sales	-	-	-	-	-	-	-	-	-	-	-	-	-	-
Contingencies														
Other Income / (Costs)	-	-	-	-	-	-	-	-	-	-	-	-	-	-
Exceptional income / (costs)	-	-	-	-	-	-	-	-	-	-	-	-	-	-
Reorganisation Costs	-	-	-	-	-	-	-	-	-	-	-	-	-	-
Adjustment - Cost Reduction Programme	-	-	-	-	-	-	-	-	-	-	-	-	-	-
Debtors and prepayments - Days outstanding (S	-	-	-	-	-	-	-	-	-	-	-	-	-	-
Other debtors - CCY mm	-	-	-	-	-	-	-	-	-	-	-	-	-	-
Inventory - Days outstanding (COS)	-	-	-	-	-	-	-	-	-	-	-	-	-	-
Other current assets	-	-	-	-	-	-	-	-	-	-	-	-	-	-
Accounts payable - Days outstanding (COS)	-	-	-	-	-	-	-	-	-	-	-	-	-	-
Accrued liabilities - CCY mm	-	-	-	-	-	-	-	-	-	-	-	-	-	-
Suppliers of Fixed Assets	-	-	-	-	-	-	-	-	-	-	-	-	-	-
Other current liabilities	-	-	-	-	-	-	-	-	-	-	-	-	-	-
Change in Working Capital	-	-	-	-	-	-	-	-	-	-	-	-	-	-
Other long-term assets	-	-	-	-	-	-	-	-	-	-	-	-	-	-
Other long-term liabilities (net)	-	-	-	-	-	-	-	-	-	-	-	-	-	-
Risk reserves and provisions increased / (release	-	-	-	-	-	-	-	-	-	-	-	-	-	-
Capital expenditures	-	-	-	-	-	-	-	-	-	-	-	-	-	-
Depreciation - Fixed Assets	-	-	-	-	-	-	-	-	-	-	-	-	-	-
Amortisation - Intangible Assets	-	-	-	-	-	-	-	-	-	-	-	-	-	-
Asset sale proceeds	-	-	-	-	-	-	-	-	-	-	-	-	-	-
Asset sale - NAV	-	-	-	-	-	-	-	-	-	-	-	-	-	-
Current Asset Add-Back	-	-	-	-	-	-	-	-	-	-	-	-	-	-
Issue of common stock	-	-	-	-	-	-	-	-	-	-	-	-	-	-
Dividend on common (payout ratio)	-	-	-	-	-	-	-	-	-	-	-	-	-	-
Extraordinary items (cash)	-	-	-	-	-	-	-	-	-	-	-	-	-	-

Glossary

Accession agreement – An agreed form of document whereby a new partner may be admitted to the transaction on the same terms as the original parties.

Business plan – A substantial document prepared by management which gives a broad description and history of the business, its past trading record and the basis on which the business will be operated in the future. It will also contain the financial projections for the business which will be incorporated in the model (see below). This document and the model will be heavily relied upon by the equity providers and bankers and will be the subject of warranties by management.

Certain funds period – The date from the making of the offer to a longstop date, normally being the period necessary to complete the compulsory purchase procedure (see below). This term is used in the banking arrangement as, under the City Code on Takeovers and Mergers, the investment banker advising the bidding vehicle must confirm the availability of funds to complete the offer.

Come along rights (also known as drag along rights) – Rights, usually contained in the articles of association of the company, under which, when shareholders, usually holding a majority of the shares, wish to sell to a third party, the remaining shareholders are bound to sell on the same terms. (See also *tag along rights*.)

Compulsory purchase procedure – The provisions of sections 429 and 430 of the Companies Act 1985 under which, in general terms, when 90 per cent of the shares for which an offer has been made have been the subject of acceptances, the balance of the shares may be acquired compulsorily on the same terms.

Conditions precedent (CPs) – Conditions which must be satisfied before a contract or agreement can be effective. Particularly relevant in relation to MBOs as the banks will insist on numerous CPs being satisfied on a variety of matters (e.g. security, production of due diligence reports) at different stages of the transaction.

Disclosure letters – Both in respect of the investment agreement with the equity house and the banking arrangements the MBO team will be warranting the due diligence reports on the business. There will be additional matters or changes of which the MBO team may wish to inform the other parties before the transaction proceeds so as to avoid potential warranty liability. These will be disclosed in appropriate disclosure letters.

Drag along rights – See *come along rights*.

Envy ratio – An internal ratio used by the equity house or venture capitalists to compare the extent to which the management team is investing on a more beneficial basis, normally because of the gearing effect of subordinated loans being made by the equity house. Usually calculated by grossing up on the one hand the equity house's investment from its actual equity percentage to 100 per cent and on the other hand doing the same for the MBO team's investment and showing one as the multiple of the other.

Equity kicker – Sometimes funds may be lent to an MBO vehicle which, because of their risk, are compensated on the upside with a return which bears a relationship to the results of the business. Such additional return is often colloquially known as an equity kicker. (See also *mezzanine finance*.)

Exit – The term applied to the event by which the equity house will realize its investment in the MBO. This will normally be by one of the following routes:

- a flotation (listing of the business) on an appropriate stock exchange;
- a trade sale of the business; or
- a recapitalization of the business (secondary MBO).

Flotation – The listing of a business on the Stock Exchange giving a quotation for its shares. Also known as an *initial public offering (IPO)*.

Give-away ratio – An internal ratio used by the equity house. This normally compares the internal rate of return (IRR) projected on the equity house's investment with the IRR available on the total equity.

Headroom – A term used by accountants and bankers which describes the amount of unused banking facilities at a particular time by comparing the total amounts drawn with the total facilities available.

Inducement fee – Because of the risk of a third party intervening in an MBO with a higher price and in the light of the considerable potentially abortive work which will be undertaken by the equity house, it will normally seek a fee from the target business in such circumstances as a form of compensation. This is known as an inducement fee and is usually part of the *non-solicitation agreement* (see below). Note 1999/10 from the Panel on Takeovers and Mergers indicates that such fees should be *de minimis* and not normally exceed 1 per cent of the offer value. Furthermore, such arrangements should be fully disclosed in the offer document and should be on display.

Initial public offering (IPO) – See *flotation*.

Internal rate of return (IRR) – The rate expressed as an annual percentage which, applied as a discount to all of the cash flows of the business (whether received or paid), gives a value of zero when such discounted cash flows are aggregated together.

Irrevocable undertaking – In a public takeover transaction, a commitment by a shareholder to accept the offer. To be secure from the offeror's point of view, the commitment should be irrevocable, i.e. the shareholder must not be able to change his mind. Some undertakings are nowadays revocable if a higher offer emerges after a certain period of time or if a higher offer emerges which is in excess of certain pre-agreed margins above the original offer.

Junior debt – Debt which is lower in terms of priority of security and repayment than other classes of debt. (See also *senior debt*.)

Loan to value ratio (LTV) – A term used in banking documentation to define a covenant whereby the outstanding amount of a loan is not to exceed a predetermined percentage of the value of the borrower's assets (normally its properties).

Management buyout (MBO) – A transaction under which the management of a listed company or a subsidiary or group of subsidiaries acquire the business either from the public shareholders (see *public to private*) or from the parent company. NB: Other variants exist, e.g. MBI (management buy-in) where external management buy into a business and existing management stand aside.

Mezzanine finance – Intermediate finance which stands between the risk equity (or ordinary shares) and the senior debt which is usually provided by the banks. The terms of the debt will have to be especially negotiated and will reflect a higher interest rate to reflect the risk and may also include in part an equity return (an equity kicker).

Model – The model is the name given to the financial appraisal of the MBO. This is a key, if not *the* key, document in the MBO process and will have to be warranted by management for its accuracy. It will contain in broad terms:

- financial projections for the trading of the business for at least the next five years;
- the financial structure of debt and equity under which the MBO will be undertaken; and
- projections as to how and over what timescale the debt will be repaid and the equity house will obtain its exit.

The model will be annexed to and form part of the *business plan*.

No embarrassment clause – Often under the MBO arrangements the equity house will give management the opportunity under an option agreement to acquire its holding. To prevent management making a quick profit ('turn') in a short period by buying and reselling the holding (probably by flotation), management will be committed to a no embarrassment clause where part of the profit in such circumstances must be paid to the equity house.

Non-solicitation agreement – An agreement whereby the target company undertakes to the equity house not to solicit or initiate an offer from any other party for the company or its subsidiaries during the currency of the negotiations. Usually part of *inducement fee* arrangements.

Pre-emption right – An obligation usually contained in the articles of association of a company whereby a shareholder wishing to sell shares in the company must first offer them on equivalent terms to other members or classes of members in the company.

Promoter – In the context of an MBO a term applied to the members of the MBO team, and sometimes more specifically to the leading members of the team.

Public to private – The name given to an MBO where management buy a publicly listed company from its shareholders by way of a public offer and subsequently delist the company from the stock market.

Ratchet – The arrangement (usually contained in the articles of association of the bidding company) under which the equity house agrees to cede a proportion of the shares which it owns in the bidding company to the MBO team if the returns available to it exceed certain predetermined rates (usually expressed in terms of IRR).

Recapitalization – In the context of the MBO the name given to a transaction where the business which is the subject of the MBO is 're-geared' (i.e. takes on additional debt) to repay an equity investor, usually the equity house. In some ways this can be regarded as a second stage MBO. The extra borrowings are supported by the assets and cash flow of the business. The MBO team's percentage share of equity in the business will be increased by such a transaction.

Revolving credit facility (RCF) – An RCF or 'revolver' is a bank loan under which funds are committed by the bank or banks within certain limits and for a fixed length of time. As long as no default occurs the borrower may repay and redraw such loans during the period of the facility. Undrawn amounts will be subject to an annual commitment fee.

Senior debt – Debt which ranks higher in terms of priority of security and repayment than other classes of debt. (See also *junior debt*.)

Subordination deed – An agreement between lenders which governs the order in which they may be repaid and which relegates some loans behind others in terms of security when otherwise they would rank equally (*pari passu*). Also referred to as a 'deed of priorities'.

Support agreement – An agreement between a company and its subsidiaries under which the subsidiaries agree to provide funds to the parent in order to provide the latter with sufficient funds to meet its obligations, usually to the investors in the MBO.

Tag along rights – Rights usually contained in the articles of association of the company under which control of the company cannot pass to a third party unless an offer is made on the same terms to acquire any remaining shares. (See also *come along rights*.)

Warrantor – A member of the MBO team who is required to give warranties, usually to the lending banks and the equity house supporting the transaction, in respect of the accuracy of the business plan and model, the due diligence reports, information supplied and other key matters.

Wash-out clause – A clause in a loan agreement where a *WCF* (see below) cannot be drawn for a short period each year. The banks use this to try to avoid acquisition and working capital debt becoming intermingled, and to ensure that core debt reduces as planned.

Whitewash – More fully, the 'financial assistance whitewash procedure', the name given to the procedure under sections 155 to 158 of the Companies Act 1985 whereby a company can give financial assistance, including security, in respect of the acquisition of its shares which would otherwise be illegal under section 151 of that Act. The procedure requires the conversion of a public company to a private one under section 53 of the Act, statutory declarations of solvency by all the directors and a report by the auditors, and the passing of a special resolution.

Working capital facility (WCF) – Usually a part of the RCF which is made available to the business in respect of its day-to-day business requirements. This is particularly relevant prior to the whitewash procedure being effected.